THE BATTLE OF
CHINNBROOK WOOD

Born in Warwickshire, England, W.J. Corbett joined the Merchant Navy as a galley-boy when he was sixteen and saw the world. Later, during National Service, he became an Army Physical Training Instructor. Now living in Birmingham, the author has also worked as a factory hand, furniture-mover, building-site labourer and dishwasher. His first book, the *Song of Pentecost*, won the prestigious Whitbread Award.

'Mr Corbett has wit, originality and economy with words which put him straight in the very top class of all . . . beside the authors of such classics as *The Wind in the Willows*, *The Jungle Book* and *Black Beauty*.'

Auberon Waug

D0774620

Also by W.J. Corbett and published by Hodder

Hamish
The Dragon's Egg

Other titles

The Song of Pentecost
Winner of the Whitbread Award
Pentecost and the Chosen One
Pentecost of Lickey Top
The End of the Tale, and Other Stories
The Bear Who Stood on his Head
Dear Grumble
Toby's Iceberg
Little Elephant
Duck Soup Farm

THE BATTLE OF
CHINNBROOK WOOD

W. J. CORBETT

Illustrated by Korky Paul

*Hodder
Children's
Books*

a division of Hodder Headline plc

First published in Great Britain in 1998
by Hodder Children's Books

10 9 8 7 6 5 4 3 2 1

A Catalogue record for this book is available from
the British Library

ISBN 0 340 69964 7

Typeset by Palimpsest Book Production Limited,
Polmont, Stirlingshire
Printed and bound in Great Britain by
Mackays of Chatham PLC, Chatham, Kent

Hodder Children's Books
a division of Hodder Headline plc
338 Euston Road
London NW1 3BH

Contents

1 The Bryants at home   1

2 The Dingles Divide   17

3 The Crabtrees at home   24

4 Val gathers her forces   33

5 The enemies clash at school   45

6 Mission by owl-light   60

7 The Crabtrees under fire   72

8 A threat becomes reality   81

9 A wary truce   91

10 Emergency Action Stations   104

11 Black Saturday   113

12 Nail-biting Sunday   128

13 Crunch Monday   138

14 A fair and handsome cop   156

15 A stroll through The Secret Wood   167

THE SECRET WOOD

'Once here we lay amongst the tiger-grass,
Ferocious times.
We drove our glittering spears deep home
A reed-shower cutting shadows down,
Our youth in arms'

Joe Crabtree

One

The Bryants At Home

'Someone's pinched my left rollerskate,' announced Val, gliding into the kitchen on her right one. 'I only took them off for a minute to dash into the corner shop. I gave a tied-up alsatian dog a toffee to guard them for me. But when I came out it was gone.'

'What, the alsatian was gone?' grinned Bob, her brother. 'So the police will be looking for a skating alsatian dog chewing a toffee. Did anyone notice which paw he skated away on? That could be a vital clue!'

'It's not funny,' snapped Val. 'The alsatian dog was still there but my skate was gone.'

'You should have tied the skates around your neck,' said Mrs Bryant, too busy to look up. 'Trusting an alsatian to guard anything is asking for trouble. And don't wear that skate in my kitchen unless you're prepared to mop up the trackmarks. These are new tiles.'

'I've got another joke Val will hate,' said Bob. He was hunched over the kitchen table wolfing down the remains of last night's pizza. He looked up, congealed cheese and tomato dripping disgustingly from his chin. 'A few minutes ago I looked out of our front window and guess what I saw?'

'Your ugly face reflected,' scowled Val.

'Will you please take your quarrels elsewhere,' said their weary mother as she topped and tailed and peeled carrots. 'I'm trying to prepare a casserole for dinner. We'll be making do with cheese sandwiches tonight if you don't get from under my feet. And your father won't take kindly to making do with sandwiches after a hard day at his bank!'

'Anyway, I saw . . .' said Bob, grinning at Val, 'a certain someone whizzing past our house on a skate like yours with a bit of plywood on top. And guess who that someone was?'

'Billy Crabtree, who else?' said Val, bitterly. 'Why does his horrible family steal other people's property?'

'Maybe because they have so little themselves,' mused Mrs Bryant. 'But that's no excuse, I know.'

'Too right it's no excuse!' shouted Val. She glared at Bob. 'It was Billy Crabtree, then?'

'Only the village tearaway himself,' Bob grinned.

'That awful boy,' cried Val, stamping her skating foot on the kitchen floor and flinging mud everywhere.

'In the cupboard there's a mop and a bucket to clean up that mess when your tantrum is over,' said her mother, pointing. 'And you'll find a scrubbing brush!'

Angry as she was, Val went down on her hands and knees and scrubbed the kitchen floor.

'There's a good girl. It's the way I've brought you up,' Mrs Bryant smiled through her tears as she peeled onions. 'Though you can be a snobby madam at times.'

'And you are too tolerant, Mum,' complained Val. 'I've noticed you always side with the Crabtrees. If you were a caring mother you'd storm around to the Crabtree house and demand my left skate back. You seem so unmotherly sometimes, Mother. I wouldn't be surprised if you patted Billy Crabtree on the back for stealing my skate!'

'Don't exaggerate, dear,' said Mrs Bryant, slicing a leek. 'But it's true, I do like the Crabtree children. Especially Joe. He offered to mow our lawn last week and kindly presented me with my favourite rose-trowel that had been missing for ages. He found it on the village rubbish-dump where I must have discarded it with my wheelbarrow of rubbish by mistake.'

'Where Billy hid it, you mean,' said Val, scornfully. 'Joe Crabtree always covers up for his thieving brother. It was probably Joe who taught Billy the ropes of stealing.'

'You're wrong about Joe,' said Bob. 'He's no more a thief than we all are in our wilder moments. He scrumps apples and plums from people's gardens, but who doesn't? Anyway, it's a known fact that Billy only borrows things. They always come back by way of the rubbish-dump sooner or later.'

'Joe Crabtree is just the chief thief holding those children in his clutches,' Val scoffed. 'I'll bet they all dance around him singing "gotta picka pocket or two" like in the *Oliver* film.'

'You've got Joe quite wrong,' interrupted her mother. 'After he'd cut our grass he gave me a lovely poem he had written. It was about a hedgehog who had lost all of his quills except one, and how the poor creature learned to cope with the teasing from the bullies. It was very moving. Joe told me that when he grows up he's going to be a famous writer to help his mum pay the bills. I think that's a lovely thing for a son to say. It can't be easy for that young boy having to be dad to five brothers and sisters, now their real dad is dead.'

'I'll do the same for you when my band hits the big-time, Mum,' promised Bob. 'Our own dad will probably be made redundant from his bank at the exact moment our band's first disc goes platinum.'

'I've always wanted a gold-plated zimmer-frame,' smiled Mrs Bryant. 'And your dad has always wanted more time to talk to his beloved grapevine in the greenhouse.'

'Weasel words, Mum,' scoffed Val. 'Bob lives in the same dreamworld as Joe Crabtree. We all know that Bob will follow his dad into some dreary bank. As for Crabtree, he'll be needing every penny he earns just to pay all the fines to keep his family out of prison. For myself, I wouldn't glance at any poem of his.'

'Joe blushed and stammered when your name was mentioned,' said Mrs Bryant, slyly. 'Though I can't see much to blush over while you're moaning and groaning about a rollerskate that will come back sooner or later.'

'That's true,' said Bob. 'When Billy tires of skateboarding down hills, Joe will find the skate on the rubbish-dump and bring it back in the dead of night. Yet why he should fancy Val beats me. I can't see the attraction myself. He'd soon get fed up if he had to live with her every day.'

'I don't believe this!' yelled Val. 'Am I the only Bryant who can see the cunning beneath the Crabtree charm?'

'You're more than half-cunning yourself, young lady,' said her mother. 'A bit of humility would do you no harm. Think yourself lucky we're not as poor as the Crabtrees. Be grateful that you have a father who earns good money to buy us our luxuries.'

'I second that,' said Bob. 'Dad does a thankless

job in difficult times. Everyone hates bank managers but he still brings home the bacon. When I'm rich and famous and living in New York hotels I'll retire him. Then he can spend the rest of his life talking to his vine that has never produced a grape.'

'Not forgetting his beloved train-set in the attic,' smiled Mrs Bryant. 'It's long been his dream to dust it off and get the signals working.'

'Who cares about luxuries,' said Val, impatiently. 'My only ambition is the article I want to write for the school magazine. My project is about The Secret Wood and the ancient cherry-tree that grows there. The tree is enormous and hollow and I'm convinced it hides an historical secret. The story goes that, back in the mists of time . . .'

'Oh no, not that again,' groaned Bob, coring a red pepper for his mum. 'It's just an old hollow tree filled with leaves and the skeletons of owls and the odd dormouse who forgot to wake up.'

'If I may finish,' said Val, primly. 'Mum is interested, even if you aren't. You see, Mum, the legend goes back to the Dark Ages when a king scrambled into the branches of the cherry-tree to escape his wife, who was chasing him with a golden rolling-pin. His name was King Fred The Fearful and his wife, Queen Gertie, was chasing him because he'd stolen her crown and jewels to give to a lovely young maiden he fancied. Now, though Queen Gertie was old and quite ugly, she was a very good tree-climber. Swarming up the cherry-tree after him, she clocked King Fred with her golden rolling-pin until he fell into a deathly faint. The loyal courtiers promptly chopped off Queen Gertie's head for daring to slay their king. But the golden rolling-pin was never found. I have a theory that I intend to explode in the next issue of the school magazine. I believe that Queen Gertie clubbed the king to death and slipped the murder weapon down into the hollow of the cherry-tree. She was trying to hide the evidence, you see, though it did her little good. And I am certain that in the hollow bowels of the ancient cherry-tree the murder weapon still lies after all those centuries. That is my theory after reading Professor Wally's learned book, and I intend to prove it.'

'Rubbish,' said Bob, his patience gone. 'You and your Professor Wally have got your kings mixed

up. It was King Charles who shinned up a tree, and that was an oak. And he wasn't hiding from Queen Gertie, but from the Roundhead soldiers, everyone knows that!'

'King Charles wasn't the only king who climbed trees,' snapped Val. Then she looked worried. 'But there's a very big problem, Mum.'

'What's that, dear?' soothed her mother, though she could have guessed. 'It's the bridge in The Dingles I need to cross to carry out my project,' said Val.

'Ah, that bridge,' sighed Mrs Bryant. 'It was the cause of many troubles when I was young. Don't tell me, the kids who live on the other side won't give you right of way. Anyone in particular?'

'The Crabtrees,' said the angry girl. 'And Joe in particular.'

'Joe!' said Mrs Bryant, surprised. 'He seems like such a nice lad, and he certainly likes you.'

'Not when it comes to projects he doesn't, for he's doing one too,' said Val bitterly. 'Probably for sheer spite he's also writing an article for the school magazine. He intends to say that historical researchers like me should be banned from The Secret Wood because our tramping feet will destroy the delicate balance of nature. He says I'll frighten the animals and his precious yellow-hammer birds who live there. And what can I do, when he and his family control the bridge and The Secret Wood that lies on their side of The Dingles? The Crabtrees are so wild and powerful, Mum.'

'It's always been that way,' remembered Mrs Bryant. 'The Dingles area being so long and narrow and the bridge cutting the land in two always caused fights and arguments.'

'Joe is probably just putting the frighteners on,' said Bob. 'The Crabtrees won't let Val and her rich pals cross the bridge because they don't like their snooty ways. And I don't blame Joe and his family at all. When did Val and Angela and Cyril last offer the Crabtree kids a ride on their new bikes? Never, that's when. That's why Billy borrows things, because he can't get a legal lend of them. Of course, it all means nothing to me. I haven't felt a twinge of snobbery since I joined my band as bass guitarist. Everyone's equal in the pop business.'

'And very talented you sound, dear,' said his mother, proudly. 'Your father thinks so too, even though he does shake his fist about the din coming from the spare bedroom.'

'How about my talent?' wailed Val. 'How can I do my research in The Secret Wood when the Crabtrees won't let me in to take notes and measure things? Yesterday Josie Crabtree cornered me in the school corridor and warned me to keep my stuck-up nose to this side of the bridge. I'm not stuck-up, am I, Mum?'

'Only a bit, dear,' said her mother, smiling. 'But I really think you should be trying to make friends with the Crabtrees instead of antagonising them.'

'Never,' vowed Val. 'I have my pride.'

'So have the Crabtrees,' said Bob.

Mrs Bryant popped her casserole and an apple-pie into a slow oven. 'Val, dear, if you think your article for the school magazine is important, you must swallow your pride and talk things over with Joe. This feud is probably making him just as unhappy as you are.'

'I will never bow and scrape to a Crabtree,' said Val, defiantly.

'In that case, I can say no more,' said Mrs Bryant, sadly.

'I've got something to say, Mum,' said Bob, licking his lips. 'When will the special casserole and apple-pie be done? When will it start smelling like it's dying to be scoffed?'

'Exactly one minute before your father gets home,' said his mum, wagging a finger. 'And not one second sooner.'

'In that case I'll try to last out on cheese sandwiches and pickle,' said Bob. 'With mustard.'

'And you?' Mrs Bryant asked her daughter.

'I refuse to eat until my left skate comes back,' said Val, stubbornly.

'You could be waiting a long time,' warned Bob. 'It all depends on how soon Billy gets tired of skateboarding and flings it on the rubbish-dump for Joe to bring back. You could be as thin as a rake by then.'

'If you were a proper brother you'd fight the Crabtrees for me,' said Val, savagely.

'What, over a skate and some silly article in the school magazine?' said Bob. 'I've more important things to do. Like helping to launch my band, The Tumbling Housebricks, and studying the pop-charts.'

'Coward!' shouted the girl.

'Right, I think I've heard enough of your arguments,' said Mrs Bryant. She reached into a cupboard. Turning, she brandished a rolling-pin. 'Now this might not be golden like Queen Gertie's, but it's just as effective. So, are you going to sit down to a civilised lunch or not? Otherwise I might decide to crack a couple of silly heads.'

Val shrugged. 'I might be able to force down a wafer-thin cheese sandwich with a hint of pickle.'

'Thick bread and cheese, the lot, for me, Mum,' said Bob, hungrily. 'And a jar of beetroot if you've got one.'

'I'll tell you what I'll do,' said Mrs Bryant to her daughter. 'If I see Joe in the village I'll have a quiet word about your missing skate. On the other hand he might call round this weekend to ask if our lawn needs cutting again. If he does you can saunter into the garden wearing your nice new frock and make some friendly conversation about your articles for the school magazine. There might even be a meeting of minds. Joe can be very charming if you give him a chance.'

'He'll never get the chance to charm me,' retorted Val. 'Anyway, who wants to listen to boring hedgehog poems, and about stupid yellow-hammers?'

'And who wants to hear you banging on about Queen Gertie and her golden rolling-pin?' mocked Bob.

'Horrible Crabtrees!' scowled Val, viciously stabbing her fork into the pickle jar. 'Making people's lives a misery!'

'By the way,' said their mother, remembering something. 'Why aren't you two in school today? It's only Friday. Not another day off for no reason?'

'Actually the classrooms have been invaded by torrents of mice,' explained Bob. 'The Pest Control man wanted us out of the way while he went about his deadly work.'

'Why couldn't he do it during the weekend?' said Mrs Bryant, puzzled. 'Because he's taking his family to the seaside this weekend,' said Val. 'And he said he and his family are entitled to enjoy the weekend just like anyone else.'

'I suppose he is,' said Mrs Bryant, bemused. 'In fact I'm certain he is . . .'

It was well past midday on that Friday when the three sat down to share a late lunch and to chat and to argue as families do . . .

Two

THE DINGLES DIVIDE

The people of Chinnbrook Wood were lucky to have lots of places to walk their dogs, to gossip in the fresh air, to enjoy picnics. Orderly people preferred the park with its paved paths and benches and plenty of litter-bins. Here dogs were allowed, though only on leads. However it was strictly forbidden to sit on the billiard-table grass. The orderly people didn't mind. They were content to sit on the benches, dog-leads looped around their ankles, simply enjoying looking at things. They especially liked to peer at the shrubs and flower-beds, listening politely as the park-keeper proudly reeled off the Latin name of every plant. He was wasting his breath. The orderly people were keen gardeners and knew much more Latin than he did. When his back was turned they cunningly snipped cuttings from his rare alpine plants to bed in their own rockeries.

At the centre of the park was a lake. It had long been a favoured place for boating and swimming. But, like the grass, now the lake could only be looked at. Three years before, a skein of Canadian geese had flown in to test the water, never to leave. When their numbers began to dwindle just before each Christmas, The Royal Society for the Protection of Birds stepped in. After a lot of banner-waving from boaters and swimmers – to no avail – the lake was declared a holy place for Canadian geese. This meant that humble English moorhens and ducks were bullied aside, forced to potter in the muddy surrounds of the lake. But the orderly people hardly noticed the changes as they sat on the benches munching their brown-bread sandwiches. They were happy to watch their children skip-rope on the tarmac paths – all the while warning that to step on to the hallowed grass would result in a ten-pound fine that would come out of their pocket-money. Most pleasing of all for the orderly people was the absence of riff-raff. The park-keeper frowned on whooping kids in scruffy tee-shirts and scuffed trainers who acted out fantasies that had no logical start, no middle, no end. Their absence from the park was part ban, but mostly choice.

Adventurous kids hated the park and its DO NOT signs and its waddling, over-protected geese. They were loyally backed by their adventurous dogs who hated everything their owners hated. Faithful to the last drop of mongrel blood they would bare their yellow teeth at the sight of a Canadian goose, or growl at an orderly person who suggested they should be wearing a lead . . .

So much for the park . . .

Also in easy reach of Chinnbrook Wood was the Common. Sporty people had long ago taken it over. Every weekend and holiday, its springy turf was packed with footballers and rugby players all sweating and bellowing like bulls. Tennis balls hissed through the air, and the cries of 'howzzat' set the pecking wood-pigeons and the rooks to startled flight. Not surprisingly, the Common held little interest for adventurous kids and dogs who dared to hunt tigers. The Common was also flat and treeless to the point of dreariness. There was not one hill to peer over and spy on a savage tribe drumming up the courage to launch a new attack, not one hollow tree to shout echoes inside and startle the dozing owls up top. The only interesting feature of the Common was the Chinnbrook stream that flowed lazily across its flatlands before plunging under the Chinnbrook Road bridge, to emerge, a boiling white-water mini-Amazon into a magical place. A place where beautiful but poisonous plants smeared venom on uncovered flesh, where many of the animals were of the man-eating or blood-sucking kind . . .

This was The Dingles . . .

Here was a perfect world for kids who thrived on hardship. No boring benches or flower-beds here. A seat was a rotting log infested with biting insects. A meal for a starving explorer could be a crammed mouthful of blackberries with the hidden danger of a trapped and angry wasp. Wild flowers in The Dingles refused to grow in neat rows, but survived where they could, and all the more beautiful for the competition.

The Dingles could be cruel, but there was

kindness too. Dock leaves always grew beside nettle-beds to rub on stung legs and soothe away the pain. And there was always the cold racing stream to numb the agony of a blistered heel. The Dingles and its captive kids loved and respected each other.

Through generations, the Dingles kids had grown to learn the tricks this magic place could tease them with. They knew that the creepy stands of fleshy plants that oozed spit made perfect pea-shooters. But there were dangers even the keenest eye could miss. Slimy green ponds were usually curtained by lush grass and flowers to make cunning traps for the slipping unwary child – to the merriment of the frogs and the newts and one's friends. These were tests of courage the true explorer faced bravely – for a child of the wilderness needed to be hardened against the day when a tiger might spring from the tiger-grass and end the worries of difficult homework for ever.

In The Dingles the trees grew as nature intended. Tall and fat around, five kids could barely encompass the mighty ones with linked hands. These hero trees had gnarly roots that grew above the ground, all stinky gardens of white mould and red-spotted toadstools. Many gang members had boasted to have climbed every tree in The Dingles, but they were smiled at. The truly noble trees had such smooth and slippery bark and so few low-growing branches that the best gripping shoes in the world slid downwards for want of a foothold. The greatest tree of all hid its secrets well. Its huge, towering canopy forever remained a mystery to generations of upturned, squinting eyes. Legend abounded that in its leafy heights lived the great-grandson of King Kong. There was proof of this. At night many restless children swore they had heard him roaring and beating his chest beneath the moon. Of all the Dingles kids, only one could have confirmed or denied their claims – a boy who in all modesty and without an audience had climbed to almost the very top of that giant tree. But Joe Crabtree, being Joe Crabtree, said little . . .

But it was always the fast stream that drew exploring souls like a magnet. Flowing deep, and difficult to wade, it was spanned at the centre of The Dingles by an old stone bridge. In times past, many battles had been fought by opposing sides for possession of that bridge, many hands shaken after a bloody-nosed victory or defeat . . .

There would be another battle for the old stone bridge that coming weekend, and the outcome would prove to be more important than either side could imagine. But in the meantime the opposing forces remained warily apart, for trust leading to friendship takes a long time to firm . . .

Three

THE CRABTREES AT HOME

Across the bridge, on the other side of The Dingles, lived the Crabtrees. They were blamed for almost everything that went wrong or missing in Chinnbrook Wood. Having lost a husband and a dad in a tragic road accident the previous year, they were now a family of seven.

The lady of the house was Mrs June Crabtree, who cheerfully managed to keep her children fed and clothed despite the loss of an adored husband and father. Her oldest child was Joe, poet and famous tree-climber. Though not quite thirteen, he took on the duty of looking after his brothers and sisters, for he was his father's son and proud of it. Next came Josie, one year younger, red of hair and flaming of temper if annoyed. She was the natural captain of the school netball team and refused to lose either argument or match.

Another year down came Billy. He was the problem child in the Crabtree apple-barrel. Billy stole things, or, as he insisted, 'borrowed' them. It was true he always returned the pinched items, but never directly. He would leave them on the waste-ground near the village rubbish-dump when he tired of playing with them. He knew that his big brother Joe would return them to their rightful owners. But in the eyes of the outraged villagers, he was a little thief, and of that there was no doubt.

'That boy will end up in prison,' gossiped the ladies in the village shop. 'He needs a father behind him.'

Perhaps he did, but he had his mum and Joe to rely on, who tried to curb his stealing sprees and calm the anger of his victims.

Jenny was quite different. She was ten and quiet and smiled a lot, and had inherited her dark curly hair from her father. Her three loves were laying hens, handsome young policemen in uniform and Sunday School.

Jakey was the serious one. Being only seven years old didn't mean that he could be treated as a child. He scorned computer games and American action films, dismissing them as rubbish. Jakey was a dedicated reader of books. He could quote large chunks from the novels of Charles Dickens and often took on the characters of the people in the stories. Sometimes he would be the Artful Dodger, sometimes Oliver Twist, sometimes even his favourite, Mr Micawber.

Last, and youngest of all, was Christie. Though now two years old, he still clung to his comforting dummy, which he wore like a cigar in the side of his mouth. But his blue eyes were full of the wisdom of the ages as he toddled around his small world and saw the happiness in his family, content that everything was going to be all right. This Friday lunchtime he was tugging at his mother's skirt as she fried fish and chips. He was ordering that the chips should be over-cooked so that they would break crisply in two when snapped.

The Crabtrees lived in a house too small for such a large family. Their pets also took up space. There was the cat and Golly the goldfish in his monster bowl on the sideboard, plus a huge smelly dog called Buff whose favourite hobby was diving into stinking canals for no reason at all. He also chewed carpets and toes if his nose wasn't smacked. Outside in the small backyard strutted seven hens and a noisy cockerel. Their lives and well-being were in the hands of Jenny, who scolded them sometimes but always thanked them for their eggs. So, in spite of the cramped conditions, the Crabtrees and their pets muddled along in a happy, free-range way.

The family stayed close and were fiercely protective of each other. When they felt down, there was always Christie to cheer them up, for he was the apple of everyone's eye . . . 'Who's the most special person in the world, Christie?' they would ask, knowing his answer.

'He is,' Christie would reply, pointing his dummy-cigar at smelly Buff who watched his little master like a hawk. Biscuit-coloured Buff loved Christie even more than he loved a meaty bone. Though he would joyously bark and lick everyone, his fierce protection of his small charge was never challenged.

As Friday lunch got underway Billy arrived

home with a rollerskate and a piece of hardboard tucked under his arm. He was flushed and out of breath. Without a word he sat down at the big kitchen table and tucked into his fish and chips. He looked the picture of innocence.

'So, Billy, where did the skate come from?' asked his worried mum. 'It looks brand-new to me.'

'And where's the other one?' said Joe. 'I suppose you've been borrowing again.'

'I only needed one skate,' explained Billy, munching his chip-butty. 'I left an alsatian dog guarding the other. I reckon I've skateboarded down every hill in Chinnbrook Wood this morning. It's good training for when I get a multi-gear mountain bike. I'll be able to afford one and things for us all quite soon.'

'Who does the skate belong to, Billy?' asked his weary mum. 'It is going back, I hope? And what's this nonsense about being able to afford expensive things?'

'When I've finished my fish and chips I'm going over to the waste-ground with my device,' said Billy, mysteriously. 'My device isn't borrowed but bought with savings money. From Mr Philips in the High Street.'

'Mr Philips who runs the Army and Navy Store?' said Josie, astonished. 'What does he sell but old junk?'

'There's money in old junk,' said Billy, pinching chips from other plates. 'And one day Mum will be proud of me.'

'I'll be proud of you when you return that skate,' scolded his mother. 'I'll be even prouder of you when you stop borrowing other people's things.'

'Joe will take care of the skate,' said Billy, dismissively. 'He'll know where to find it to take back. I'm fed up with skateboarding anyway.' He looked across the table at his big brother, confident that his latest bit of crookery would be taken care of. And so it would, for Billy felt secure in the love of his big brother . . .

Joe had taken on the father role for his brothers and sisters. He took it willingly because he knew that his mum needed help to manage. For their part, the other kids accepted Joe as the boss, for they adored him. He was already skilled at sorting out their quarrels and problems, though little more than a child himself. Mrs Crabtree quietly grieved that such a young boy should need to grow beyond his years into such responsibility. But Joe was content with his lot . . .

When his brothers were asleep in the room they shared, Joe would write poems by the light of the small bedside lamp. But that night Joe wouldn't be writing poems. He was busy composing a hard-hitting article for the school magazine concerning the protection of the countryside. He was well aware that in a house on the other side of the dividing bridge Val Bryant was also writing a piece. An article about The Secret Wood and the history of the ancient cherry-tree there. With a pen dipped in venom she would accuse Joe Crabtree of refusing her and her research group to enter the wood, to carry out vital research on the mysterious history of Queen Gertie who conked her husband to death with her golden rolling-pin. But alas, to Val's anger, The Secret Wood lay on the Crabtree side of the bridge. She had a lot of lessons to learn before she would understand why the Crabtrees would not let her and her friends cross the bridge to explore The Secret Wood. Joe would learn lessons too, in particular about the burdensome chip on his shoulder. But for the time being two opposing points of view would remain in place. The bridge would not be crossed until . . .

Joe clicked out the light and went to bed. An owl who lived in the tree outside his open window hooted softly. The boy closed his eyes and thought about the perching bird who yearned that every day could be silent night. Joe smiled in half-sleep. He was waiting for bright Saturday morning and what it might bring. Soulmates in spirit, one slept, the other ever awake . . .

Four

VAL GATHERS HER FORCES

'Are you coming with me to the bridge to back me up this morning?' said Val, confronting her brother over the breakfast table. 'Brothers are supposed to protect their sisters if danger threatens.'

'Not this one,' said Bob, wolfing scrambled eggs. 'You can fight your own stupid battles. Anyway, Angela and Cyril can be your bodyguards, they're beefy enough. I'm too busy at the moment. Me and The Tumbling Housebricks are rehearsing today. And we're hoping to record some tracks for our first album in Mick's recording-studio garage.'

'I don't know why you bother,' scoffed Val. 'There's a dozen bands in our town alone, and all much better than yours.'

'Now, you two,' warned Mrs Bryant. 'Less raised voices if you please. Your father is having a lie-in. You do remember your father? He's the one who slaves hard all week to buy you skates and guitars.'

Just then, Angela and Cyril Hopkins came riding up the drive on their new bikes. They were bought the latest model every year by their indulgent dad. They hadn't a clue or an interest in what happened to their old bikes. Perhaps they simply vanished when the bin-men arrived with the first blackbird's cheep to crush everything into their snorting machine. It never occurred to Angela and Cyril that the poor children who lived on the other side of the bridge would have given everything to own a second-hand bike. Angela and Cyril were well-fed and wore smug smiles. Angela wore her fair hair in bunches while Cyril plastered his down from a knife-edge parting. Because they were so large and rich they were treated with caution at school – which made them perfect bodyguards in Val's eyes.

'How pleased I am to see true friends,' said a relieved Val, opening the front door. 'I suppose you've heard that Billy Crabtree has stolen my left skate? But the real problem is Joe Crabtree. He's still trying to keep us out of The Secret Wood.

His latest ploy is a stupid article he's writing for the school magazine. About protecting field-mice and badgers and silly yellow-hammer birds from the damage of trampling feet. Those trampling feet being ours, who have an important mission to solve the historic mystery of the cherry-tree and the murderous Queen Gertie and her golden rolling-pin!'

'Who I believe is innocent,' said Angela, stoutly.

'Who was probably framed by the king's courtiers,' nodded Cyril.

'But where does the proof lie?' cried Val, frustrated. 'In the hollow cherry-tree, that's where. And why can't we examine the evidence? Because Joe Crabtree is denying us access to The Secret Wood.'

'Joe Crabtree is just a nature-loving anorak,' said Angela, angrily. 'How can anyone love moles more than history? I wouldn't be surprised if he collected train numbers!'

'Well,' said Val, a determined look in her eye, 'this morning we three are going to the bridge and have it out with Joe Crabtree and his horrible family. This time we'll tackle them head-on!'

'A weedy poet will be no problem,' said Cyril, squaring his shoulders.

'And Josie doesn't frighten me,' said Angela, trying to be equally brave. 'I don't care if she becomes the captain of the English netball team, she's still a nasty Crabtree to me.'

'I might as well tell you that Bob has let me down,' said Val, sadly. 'He's refused to help us. I think he sides with his mum, who likes the Crabtrees. I can't understand it at all. Can you hear them in the kitchen, those two? Bob is strumming his guitar and Mum is singing old-fashioned songs.'

'Let them strum, let them sing,' said Cyril, contemptuously. 'Let them stay in their old-fashioned world. We're living in the age of the Supernet and our dad is buying me and Angela one each to hook into.'

'My, you are lucky,' said Val, awed.

'But come on,' said Cyril, impatiently, 'let's get on our bikes and get this Crabtree business sorted out . . .'

The three pedalled down the drive and into the road, Bob's thumping beat and Mrs Bryant's

36

singing soon fading away. In two minutes they arrived at the wild and bushy entrance to The Dingles. Ever cautious, they walked their bikes through the high tiger-grass that surrounded this sacred place. The fear of past generations was theirs. A flash of tawny stripes, a raking claw . . . who knew . . . ?

On their bikes again, they were soon skidding and bumping over the twisty track that wound towards the old stone bridge. Suddenly they braked in panic, as a shrill whistle rent the air. Their approach had been rumbled. Someone knew they were on their way. It was Billy Crabtree, perched high in a tree, using The Dingles telegraph to warn his family of approaching danger. Arriving at the bridge, the three were confronted by Joe, Josie, Jenny, Jakey and little Christie. Billy came down from his high perch to join them.

'What do you want?' shouted Josie. 'Try to cross this bridge and you're gonners. The Secret Wood is out of bounds to the likes of you.'

'So hop it,' yelled little Christie from the side of his dummy. Buff bared his yellow teeth and barked his approval.

Cyril got off his bike and walked it to the centre of the bridge. The nervous girls followed him. Leaning his gleaming machine against the low safety wall, the large boy puffed out his chest and looked menacing.

'Listen, you Crabtrees,' he shouted. 'The Dingles is a free country. If we want to cross this bridge and explore The Secret Wood we're perfectly entitled to. So, stand aside if you know what's good for you.'

'We won't ignore force if you force us to,' cried Angela. 'It's vital that Val is allowed to make a scientific examination of the ancient cherry-tree in The Secret Wood. She needs to tap its trunk for hollowness and take measurements to back up her theory about Queen Gertie and her golden rolling-pin. How can she write her article for the school magazine if you won't let her examine the evidence?'

'Joe Crabtree is just jealous that my article will be better than his,' shouted Val, flushed with anger.

'Better it might be, but not so important,' answered Joe, quietly across the divide. 'My concern is the rare plants and animals living peacefully in The Secret Wood. I won't allow people to trample through an unspoiled place just to prove some wild theory about a queen and her golden rolling-pin. And what is more . . .'

'Tell them about the yellow-hammers, Joe,' cried Jenny. 'For their eggs are sacred, just as the eggs of my hens are.'

'It's true,' said Joe. 'There's a family of rare yellow-hammers nesting in the gorse bushes beside the cherry-tree. So far this year they've been undisturbed, and left alone they'll remain!'

'Sing us the yellow-hammer song, Christie,' encouraged Josie. 'The song you sing before you go to sleep.'

'A-little-bit-of-bread-and-no-cheese . . .' warbled Christie in a sweet voice from the side of his dummy.

'And what else will you say to these trespassers, Christie?' said Billy, egging his little brother on.

'Hop it!' Christie shouted to the loud barks of Buff.

'And don't think the police will help you,' shouted Jakey, the Dickens scholar. 'For the law is an ass.'

'Right,' cried Cyril, fiercely, 'if you won't listen to reason then we'll have to change your minds. Come on, Ang . . . Val . . .' and he advanced across the bridge towards the Crabtree clan . . .

Though slighter of build than Cyril, Joe stood his ground. Toe to toe, Cyril threw a punch, which Joe nimbly ducked. Then Joe swung his own fist, catching the big boy flush on the nose. Cyril howled with pain and staggered back. In the meantime Josie and Angela were having a slapping match, plus a bit of hair-pulling.

Val nervously stood back. She enjoyed a good argument, but she hated fighting. Jenny and Jakey and Christie urged their brother and sister on, while Buff circled, snapping at any heel that didn't belong to a Crabtree.

While all this was going on, Billy had seized his opportunity to sneak to the centre of the bridge. Seconds later he was wheeling Cyril's bike away, his face a picture of innocence as he passed the group of fighters. He felt no shame, though he should have done. He felt no guilt, though he reeked of it. He was hurrying away on an object of desire. Tired of skateboarding, he was taking up cycling. And only on the latest model of bike with stacks of gears to explore . . .

'Had enough?' said Joe, breathing heavily and standing back. Cyril had. But then he made a grave mistake. Tenderly fingering his bloody nose, he began to insult the proud Crabtrees – and on their own territory too.

'I know why you hate us,' he shouted. 'It's because we're rich and our parents buy us bikes and skates and things. Well, it isn't our fault that you have nothing. If you're so jealous, me and Ang have lots of old clothes and toys you can have. Just step aside and let us cross the bridge – as we're perfectly entitled to do as law-abiding children.'

Joe looked at Josie. His sister (who had just finished slapping Angela's face to a bright plum colour) looked at her brother. There was no need for words. Helped by Jenny and Jakey, they seized Cyril and hauled him to the centre of the bridge. With a heave they sent him tumbling and yelling into the cold waters below.

'Murderers,' screamed Angela. 'You've drowned my brother!'

'Glug, glug,' chuckled Christie, standing tip-toe to gaze down into the stream.

'Drowned him . . . rubbish,' said Josie, coolly. 'The water is only knee-deep. We're just washing his insulting mouth out. Now you can drag him out and take him back to where he belongs.'

'Savages,' wept Val. 'The Headmaster will be hearing about this on Monday morning, Joe Crabtree. I'll also be telling him about the article you won't let me write for the school magazine. I mean my important history article about The Secret Wood, not about boring yellow-hammers and buttercups. Perhaps you don't know, but our Headmaster used to be a history teacher before he went old and grey and stern. He'll back my Queen Gertie project, just you wait and see.'

Meanwhile Angela had slithered down the bank of the stream to help her spluttering brother from the water. Back at the centre of the bridge the fuming three reached for their bikes. Cyril had a problem.

'Where's my bike?' he yelled at the Crabtrees. 'Where's that thieving Billy? I know he's pinched it, as he pinches everything else.'

'And where's my rollerskate while we're about it,' cried Val. 'I know your Billy coaxed it from the alsation dog outside the shop.'

'So Billy borrows things, and we know it's wrong,' said Joe, coolly. 'You'll get back the bike and the rollerskate, I'll see to that.'

'The nerve of you awful people,' gasped Val, disbelievingly. 'Have you no shame at all?'

'You'd better know my dad is a solicitor,' said the furious Cyril. 'When I tell him what's happened he'll get in touch with his friend the Chief Inspector and your Billy's feet won't touch the ground. Your thieving brother will be brought to justice before The Juvenile Bench for grand theft.'

'Our dad will also get Joe jailed for attempting to drown Cyril,' shouted Angela. 'Then he won't have The Secret Wood and his precious yellow-hammers to protect against genuine historians.'

'You're wrong,' said Jakey, wisely. 'Your charges won't stick, for the law is an ass. I know because I've read all about it.'

'All this fuss about an article in the school magazine,' said Jenny, shaking her dark curls. 'All because our Billy likes to try out the latest rollerskates and bikes. All because our Joe and Josie gave Cyril the ducking he deserved. What we need is a handsome young policeman to stride on to the bridge and take the side of us Crabtrees.'

'So, I think we've said all we need to,' said Joe to the angry three. 'If you want to make more trouble, leave it till Monday at school.'

'Now, hop it,' rasped Christie, his dummy jutting gangster-like from the side of his mouth. Buff licked his adored master and growled at the intruders. Casting the Crabtrees filthy looks, the three from the posh side of The Dingles mounted their two bikes. With the soaking wet Cyril perched on Angela's handlebars they wobbled off home along the slippery, tree-lined track of The Dingles.

The victorious Crabtrees also turned for home, hopefully to enjoy bowls of mushy peas, plus a bone for Buff as a reward for a battle well fought. The lunch was perfect, the bone quite delicious . . .

Five

THE ENEMIES CLASH AT SCHOOL

Six o'clock on Monday morning. Only the milk-man noticed the dark-haired boy cycling along the quiet suburban road, a rollerskate slung around his neck. As the boy approached a certain house he began to circle and do wheelies, quick-braking and back-tyre skids. He was clearly enjoying himself. He might even have been showing-off to someone he hoped was watching through a window. At last he dismounted and walked the bike up the drive. Leaning it carefully against the wall, he draped the rollerskate over the handlebars. The bike and the skate looked as if they'd spent time on a rubbish-dump, clung as they were with dried grass and ashes. Giving them a quick brush-down with the sleeve of his anorak, the boy turned and quietly walked away. Only the milkman had watched him arrive, not a soul saw him depart. Joe Crabtree had kept his promise to return some stolen – borrowed – goods . . .

Nine o'clock on Monday morning and the pupils were shuffling into the gym for assembly. After a brief lecture from the Headmaster about the importance of respecting their teachers and doing their best at lessons, they sang, 'Morning Has Broken' quite sweetly, before filing away to their classrooms.

Val, Joe, Cyril and Angela happened to be in the same class that term. Once seated, Cyril glowered at the back of Joe's head, angrily sniffing through his swollen nose. Angela had freed her hair from its usual tidy bunches and was wearing it like a curtain over her face in an attempt to hide her bright-pink cheeks. Val sat opposite her hated enemy, casting him dagger looks. Joe refused to respond, averting his eyes every time she looked his way. Partly because he felt guilty about the battle on the bridge, mostly because the lesson was English Lit. and words fascinated him.

Lunchtime on Monday and the children sat in the dining-hall munching sausages and chips.

Ever conscious of her weight, Val nibbled at a salad. Through every forkful of lettuce and tomato her eyes never once left Joe, who was sitting close by. She looked triumphant and seemed to be bursting to speak. Joe ignored her and toyed with his chips, gazing out of the window. In fact he was puzzled. How could she look so smug after the fight on the bridge? What was she up to?

The answer came quickly. The Headmaster entered the dining-hall. 'Will Valerie Bryant and Joseph Crabtree please report to my office after lunch,' he said, then left.

Val was smiling like the Cheshire Cat delighting in Joe's bewilderment. The boy pushed away his half-eaten meal, his appetite gone. Like everyone in the school, he dreaded a summons to the Headmaster's office, especially when one could think of no reason why. Val seemed to know why. She continued to smile in an irritating way, enjoying her rival's discomfort.

The two exchanged not a word or glance as they stood in the corridor outside the Headmaster's office. Val was cool, Joe was fidgety.

Then the deep, dread voice sounded. 'Please come in.'

Joe was relieved to see that the Headmaster was smiling. On his desk lay last month's copy of the school magazine.

'I see you are both keen writers for the school magazine,' he said, leafing through the pages. 'And very interesting too. Now, Valerie, you asked for this interview. What's the problem?'

'Well, sir,' said Val in a rush. 'I'm planning to write an article for next month's issue. It's about the ancient legend of Queen Gertie who killed the king her husband by boffing him on the head with her golden rolling-pin. You see he'd taken all her jewels to give to a younger, much prettier maiden. The story goes that the evidence and proof of her guilt is to be found inside a cherry-tree in a secret wood in the heart of Warwickshire. Well, sir, it sounds exactly like the ancient cherry-tree in The Secret Wood in The Dingles.'

'And you need to do some research,' smiled the Headmaster. 'Well, it sounds a worthwhile project. I was a history teacher in my younger days so I can understand your enthusiasm. But tell me, where's the problem?'

'Joe Crabtree's the problem, sir,' said Val, beginning to weep.

The Headmaster looked sternly at Joe. 'And what problems are you putting in her way, Joe Crabtree? I will not tolerate bullying in my school.'

'Sir, I consider myself the guardian of The Secret Wood,' said Joe, quietly. 'Lots of rare plants and flowers grow there. It's also the home of many small animals in need of a safe refuge. It's also a favourite nesting place for a family of yellow-hammer birds who need protecting. Sir, my case is, if Valerie Bryant and her friends are allowed into the wood they will destroy the delicate balance of nature with their trampling boots and noise. That's what my article is going to be about, sir. To preserve The Secret Wood for the life that lives there. For it's well known that researchers like to dig trenches and chop down hedgrows to get at what they're searching for. They also light fires and toast sausages and play their guitars much too loud.'

'We wouldn't do those things!' said Val, indignantly. 'It's only the ancient cherry-tree me and Cyril and Angela are interested in.'

'A cherry-tree that is home for lots of small creatures,' Joe pointed out. 'And then there are the gorse-bushes that surround it. That's where the yellow-hammers live. You'd trample them down and frighten the birds to fly away for ever.'

'Yellow-hammers, eh?' said the Headmaster, interested. 'I've always been a keen bird-watcher. And you say they live and breed in your secret wood? Now that would be a sight to photograph for my bird-diary . . .'

'Actually, sir,' said Joe. 'There's a small path that winds through the wood. If people trod carefully they could take lots of close-up pictures of yellow-hammers going about their business. I'd gladly be your guide, Headmaster.'

'Why, thank you, Joseph,' said the man, pleased.

'But I thought you loved history, sir,' said Val, all teary again.

'It's true I've got a degree in history, Valerie,' was the gentle reply. 'But I'm afraid I agree with Joseph. The protection of the countryside is all important in these times of wilful destruction. I can only suggest that you two come to some sort of compromise. Get together and talk it over. Now you must excuse me, but I have to attend a meeting quite soon.'

Joe could have done the grinning as they left the Headmaster's office, but he didn't. Val's face was a study in stone as she marched ahead down the corridor. From her look and the stiffness of her back it was obvious the battle was far from over.

'It's not my fault,' called Joe. 'It was you who asked for the interview. How could I know he liked bird-watching more than history? I'll take you through The Secret Wood to study the yellow-hammers if you want. Bring Angela and Cyril. You'll find that wildlife is much more exciting than myths about golden rolling-pins.'

'I wouldn't study anything with you,' snapped Val over her shoulder. 'I hope your precious yellow-hammers fall off their perches as you'll be falling off yours when I'm finished. I won't say I loathe you because you know that already.'

The rest of that day at school was even more uncomfortable for Joe. He took no comfort in winning yet another battle he had not wished to fight. All through the afternoon lessons, Val, Cyril and Angela glared at him. During breaks between classes they gathered to whisper. They were talking about him, of course. He was very relieved when it was time to go home.

'Can you believe it?' cried Val to her mother who was pounding and peppering a steak for her husband's dinner. 'Our Headmaster, who has a degree in history, sided with Joe Crabtree! And all because of some stupid yellow-hammer birds. And then he had the nerve to say that me and Joe Crabtree should get together and sort it out between us!'

'Well, he is the Headmaster, dear,' said Mrs Bryant. 'It's his job to say sensible things. Why don't you make friends with Joe? I think he's a nice lad. The problem is your attitude, my girl. If you'd just get down off your high horse . . .'

'Why not offer to treat Joe to the pictures?' suggested Bob, who was shovelling down beans on toast. 'Then, after the film you could take him for a cheeseburger and a coke in the cafe. I'd take up an offer like that, no problem. But of course, being a guitarist in an up-and-coming rock band, I get more attention from girls than I can cope with.'

'Me, treat Joe Crabtree to a night out?' shuddered Val. 'I'd sooner go out with Dracula.'

'Apart from the row over the school article, what have you got against Joe?' asked Bob. 'It isn't his fault that his brother Billy is a thief. And he brought back your skate and Cyril's bike in the dead of night. I know because I was looking out of my window seeking inspiration for a song I'm composing. In fact I think Joe is dead alright, even if he does only write about hedgehogs.'

'Jingles and rhymes,' scoffed Val.

'If you two are going to keep this up . . .' said Mrs Bryant, wearily.

The two always knew when their mother's patience was about to snap. Wisely they moved out of the kitchen to the lounge, where they could continue their argument in peace.

'I think you're making a mistake,' said Bob, idly strumming his guitar. 'Mum's right, and so is the Headmaster. Why not make friends with

Joe? He'll never change his mind about your lot roaming through The Secret Wood while you're still enemies. Just invite him down the chippie for some fish and chips.'

'All he thinks about is birds and flowers,' said Val, bitterly. 'How can you stroll down to the chippie with a boy who talks all the time about yellow-hammers?'

'Me and my band talk about birds all the time,' grinned Bob. 'Take Fiona Robson, for instance. Now she is something. She's always trying to sit in the next desk to me . . .'

But Val was already stalking off down the hall and out of the front door to cool her temper with a long bicycle ride . . .

'Listen in, you lot,' said Mrs Crabtree, clicking off the telly. 'I've been getting reports from people I meet in the shops about your behaviour over the weekend, and I want this feuding to stop.'

'Oh, Mum,' wailed Josie. 'You've switched off my favourite programme.'

'Watch my lips, young lady,' snapped her mother. 'I'm ashamed of you all. Brawling on the bridge, indeed! What would your father have thought? Do we want the police round here?'

'Hop it!' yelled Christie, astride Buff's back and aiming an imaginary uppercut at a remembered Cyril.

'Do you see?' said their mum. 'Even little Christie is growing up to believe in violence. Joe, you should be setting an example, not encouraging your brothers and sisters to fight other children. And from what I've heard, you started it!'

'I didn't,' Joe protested. 'I was attacked and forced to defend myself.'

'And I suppose you were forced to steal?' said Mrs Crabtree, looking angrily at Billy. 'I've been told that a lad's brand-new bike went missing.'

'I only borrowed it,' said Billy. 'Anyway, the gears didn't work properly. After one ride around the estate I knew it wasn't the bike for me.'

'The bike has been returned, Mum,' said Joe, quickly. 'And none the worse for wear, I promise.'

'Can you promise that nothing like this will happen again?' demanded his mother. She looked at Billy. 'All of you?'

'I don't know what all the fuss is about,' said Billy. 'It was only a bike borrowed for a bit.'

'The rows are over, Mum,' said Joe, hating to see her distressed. 'The bike and the skate have gone back to their owners, and the problem on the bridge was thrashed out in the Headmaster's office this morning. I don't think Valerie Bryant and her crowd will attempt to invade The Secret Wood again. She's all bluff.'

'You should have seen her face when she stormed back into class,' giggled Josie. 'Temper tears running down her cheeks and stamping her feet. Our Joe certainly put her in her place in the Headmaster's office.'

'Don't be unkind,' said Mrs Crabtree, sharply. 'And remember, The Secret Wood doesn't belong to you alone. And there's one more thing. The children you assaulted on the bridge could press charges. Their parents are quite influential, so I've heard.'

'I hope they send a handsome police constable to arrest us,' said Jenny, hopefully. 'One with nice blue eyes who winks at me a lot.'

'Even if the constable came, he'd be wasting his

time,' said Jakey, loftily. 'For even with a thousand clues to pin on us and Billy, he'd be stumbling in the dark. For the law is an ass, said the Beagle . . . or was it the Beadle . . . anyway, he said it in *Oliver Twist* . . .

'So they can hop it!' shouted Christie, rolling his dummy around his mouth. Buff rolled his little hero around the carpet and barked his happiness.

Quite soon the Crabtree family were sprawled over the battered three-piece suite and the carpet, enjoying baked beans and fried eggs. Jenny, who was in charge of the hens in the back garden had patted them for doing their best. Her hens always fondly obliged their small mistress . . .

'The eggs we're enjoying are newly-laid,' she said, proudly. 'So I want you to all join in with a rousing "cluck, cluck". And you'll notice that every egg is double-yolked for your enjoyment. So come on, let's hear it . . .'

'Cluck, cluck,' shouted the family, grinning and laughing as they tucked into their meal . . .

Later that night sitting close to his bedside lamp,

Joe jotted down a poem that had pushed into his head. It was about tigers and tiger-grass and the cherry-tree that grew in The Secret Wood. It was about The Dingles he stalked through, armed only with a flimsy reed spear . . .

We raised our heads
Admired the cherry-tree,
It swayed,
A million devilled earrings wet with blood . . .
We fled,
Hysterically laughing, shrill despair,
Where grows the tiger-grass expect a tiger there

Topping his biro and closing his note-pad, he checked to see that his little brothers were sleeping sound, and went to bed.

The owl on the branch outside his window hooted softly. Joe, smiling sleepily, hooted back. It was their private code. For both of them it was comforting to have friends . . .

Across the bridge a girl slept sort of soundly. Her dreams were filled with images of a boy and a girl walking hand-in-hand through a secret wood to the trilling sound of a yellow-hammer bird crouched in gorse. The girl stirred restlessly and began a more blissful dream . . . of a girl being presented with a medal for the best historical article the school had ever known. But deepest sleep obscured the end of her dream.

And then another tomorrow came and it was back to uniformed reality . . .

Six

MISSION BY OWL-LIGHT

At school the next morning, Val and Angela and Cyril ignored Joe. No hateful looks, nothing. Josie whispered to her brother that the trio had been so defeated during the battle of the bridge that they had thrown in the towel, too ashamed to tell anyone. Joe was not so sure. He was watching the way the three took every opportunity to gather together, to whisper in each other's ears. Joe sensed a plot, and it made him nervous. During the maths lesson he racked his brains for the answers to algebra puzzles, and also to the schemes that could be going on in those three, close-bent heads. Then school was thankfully over . . .

The autumn nights were drawing in. By seven o'clock it was almost dark, with a late Indian-summer mist rising from the ground from the heat of the day. It was an owl-light night . . .

In her room Val dug out her old black jeans and sweater. A dark-blue bobble hat completed the outfit. Laying it out on her bed, she went downstairs and opened the lounge door. The lights were out, the telly on.

'I'm just going to Angela's for an hour or two,' she called inside, casually. 'I promised I would and I can't let her down.'

'Don't be late home,' warned Mr Arthur Bryant, wagging a finger over the back of his armchair.

'Yes, Dad,' said Val. 'No, Dad . . .'

Back upstairs she quickly changed into her dark clothes. Then she crept softly back down the stairs and out of the back door. Angela and Cyril were waiting by the garden shed, dressed in designer-black. Cyril was wearing a balaclava and was carrying the latest torch that could make night into almost day. He looked very S.A.S.

'Are we ready?' whispered Val. 'Let's go . . .'

The road that lead to The Dingles was almost deserted. They weren't noticed as they stole along in single file. The sweeping lights of a car briefly pinned them against a hedgerow as it sped past on a mission of its own. Soon the three were squeezing through the gap in the hawthorn hedge that opened on to the tiger-grass fields of The Dingles. Guiding them, with his magic torch on pencil-beam, Cyril still managed to fall into a slimy toad-pond, causing the alarmed creatures to croak into the night. On a bough, an owl with true super-vision hooted his contempt. Moments later, Val and Angela stumbled into a bed of stinging nettles. Like Cyril, they howled as softly as they could. Yet the three marched doggedly on, ignoring the owl who seemed to be hooting his contempt from his perch. Then soon they were treading a familiar path, the path to the bridge . . .

They crawled the last few yards. It was forbiddingly eerie crossing to the Crabtree side of the bridge without being challenged. Words could not describe Val's feelings as they crept into The Secret Wood, that wonderful, fabled place. Misty moonlight filtered through the trees and bushes, dappling the mossy ground with shifting patches of light as the branches of the trees swayed in the gentle air. The Secret Wood was very creepy.

They could hear small scufflings and cheeps and grunts as their ears became attuned. Was that a badger's cough as he ambled black-and-white in the moonlight? Could that be a nightingale there, its song so sweet upon the air? And what was that? The three started, nearly bolted as the figure of a lovely lady walked across that magic sward, to disappear before their eyes amongst the moon-dappled trees as if she had never been.

'She looked just like me,' breathed Val to herself. 'Or did I look like her?'

'She was wearing a little crown on her head,' said Angela, awed. 'And the loveliest gown all trimmed with gold.'

'It's the swaying of the trees casting shadows,' hissed Cyril, impatiently. He clicked on his high-powered torch and beamed it around The Secret Wood and the spell of the ghostly lady was broken by harsh light.

'Look, the ancient cherry-tree,' whispered Angela, pointing. She was right. There in the searching light was the tree they had battled so far to see. It was so huge round its trunk, it had to be one thousand years old. It was truly a king amongst trees. In its branches hung thick bunches of succulent cherries, shining dewed black in the torchlight. Val's first impulse was to rush forward and embrace its mighty trunk, but the historian in her urged caution. Instead the three advanced in an awed way with their tape-measures and notepads to record the tree's vital statistics. While Angela held the end of the tape, Val ran around the trunk. The tape ran out before she was two thirds around. After some more shuffling and marking, they finally recorded its girth and entered it into Val's note-book. Then, reaching into the back-pocket of her jeans, Val pulled out a scientific hammer and began to tap the old, almost barkless trunk, while listening.

'Just as the legend says,' she gasped, excitedly. 'It's hollow. Now we'll climb into the branches. There's bound to be a hole into which Queen Gertie dropped her murder weapon. Remember, the golden rolling-pin was never found. Come on, Cyril, we'll need your magic torch. And Angela, you stay below and watch for wandering spirits – this is a spooky place. If you see the lady in the drifting gown, ask her if she's Queen Gertie.

Though she'll probably just moan and wring her hands, knowing ghosts . . .'

Miserably wet, but still game, Cyril clambered up the trunk of the cherry-tree behind Val. It was exactly as the girl had thought. In the middle of the tree, where the massive boughs divided, was a hollow they could peer down into. Cyril directed his torch into the gnarly innards.

'What can you see?' whispered Val.

'Dead leaves and twigs,' said Cyril. 'And a few old bones. Squirrels, probably.'

'Surely you can see something glittering,' said Val, impatiently. 'Get out of the way and let me have a look.'

'Steady,' warned Cyril, holding the back of her anorak as she leaned.

'Quiet – and flash the light around,' snapped the girl. Then she gave a low whoop. 'I can see something shining down there. I just can't make out what it is . . .'

Some two hundred metres away, Joe was gazing out of his bedroom window at the night. He enjoyed watching and listening to the wind in the trees, and there on the usual branch swayed his hooting owl friend. Then he was distracted by what looked like a light flickering in the depths of The Secret Wood. He blinked, then looked again. It was a light, no question. But who could be roaming through the wood in the dark, and why? He felt angry and protective. It was as if someone was strolling through his private world without permission.

He dressed quickly and crept along the landing to knock on Josie's bedroom door. After a few whispered words, she joined him. Soon they were racing across the road and into the trees, the owl-light moon showing the way.

'Hurry up,' hissed Angela. 'I'm frightened down here by myself. I'm sure I just saw the ghost lady gliding through the trees again.'

'You're supposed to be a scientist,' said Val, sharply. 'Spirits and ghosts won't harm you if you keep very quiet. Do some more measuring or something, me and Cyril are busy.'

'There's certainly something down there,' said Cyril, having another look. 'I can see it glittering through the piles of leaves and bones.'

'Why didn't we bring a rope and some kind of grappling hook?' said Val, vexed. 'We could have fished for Queen Gertie's golden rolling-pin right now.'

'We don't know the glitter is gold,' said Cyril. 'It could be just a shiny sweet-wrapper the wind blew in.'

'Well, there's nothing more we can do without equipment,' sighed Val. 'We'll just have to come again tomorrow night.'

'Oh no you won't,' said a quiet voice. The three scientists yelped. The two up the tree scrambled down to join Angela, who was having a fit of the trembles. Just then the shadowy figure of Joe stepped from behind some bushes, Josie close behind him.

'Of all the sneaky tricks,' gasped Val, angrily. 'You could have given us nervous breakdowns, Joe Crabtree!'

'It's you who's doing the sneaking,' blazed Josie. 'Flashing lights all over the place and disturbing the wildlife.'

'We don't care about your precious wildlife,'

snapped Val. 'We're on the verge of a major discovery. Our work is more important than shambling old badgers and a few twittering birds.'

'Well, your "work" is finished as from now,' said Joe. 'And if I ever catch you poking around in this wood without permission, you'll be in trouble.'

'Remember what happened on the bridge the other day,' said Josie. 'Consider yourselves lucky to get off much lighter this time. We could have sent Buff our hunting dog in first. He would have pinned you to the cherry-tree until morning. So now, start making tracks for home, you know the way.'

'I've never been so insulted in all my life!' said Angela, indignantly. 'England is supposed to be free, yet it seems to be ruled by the Crabtree clan.'

'Wait till our dad hears about this,' growled Cyril. 'He's an awfully powerful solicitor, you know. When he hears that you Crabtrees are stopping us roaming freely through the countryside, he'll fly up the wall and consult his legal books.'

'I'm not going to argue with you at this time of night,' said Joe, angrily. 'Just get out of this wood while you have the chance, unless you want to be forced out?' Beside him, Josie cracked her knuckles menacingly.

The angry three realised that further words were useless. Turning, they retraced their steps to the bridge. The journey back along The Dingles path seemed more difficult. Doubtless, because on the way to the wood their hopes had been high, while now on the way back they were completely crushed. Fearfully they stole through the tiger-grass in case they disturbed heaven knows what in its tall thickness. Soaking wet and nettle stung, they parted in the road outside Val's house.

In spite of the setback Val took comfort from the fact that they had made some important discoveries in The Secret Wood that night. The cherry-tree was hollow, and something golden glittered at the bottom. And who could the lady they had seen drifting through the trees be, other than the ghost of Queen Gertie? How she longed to visit that magical place again, to unlock the secrets that lay hidden in the hollow trunk. She yearned to have time to delve into the mystery of the ghostly lady. Could the strange vision be linked to the legend of the cherry-tree? But how could Val investigate these important matters, when the awful Crabtrees guarded the wood so jealously? Thinking and worrying about the problem, it was a long time before she drifted off to sleep . . .

'We were a bit hard on them, eh?' said Joe to Josie as they parted on the landing.

'I don't think so,' said the girl. 'I've got no sympathy for them at all. Unless you have for Valerie Bryant.'

'Who said so?' said Joe, colouring.

'A little bird,' grinned his sister. 'A yellow-hammer, actually.'

'Don't be daft,' said Joe, turning to go to bed. 'With her airs and graces she's more trouble than she's worth.'

The owl was there again perched in its usual spot. It hooted softly. Getting no reply, it hooted louder. Still no response. Joe was out to the world . . .

Seven

THE CRABTREES UNDER FIRE

Angela and Cyril's father was very angry. Not so much over the stealing of his son's bike, for that had come back. Mr Hopkins was angry about the theft of his valuable coin collection that hadn't come back. Four days had passed since the burglary, and the police had yet to solve the case. They knew that the thief had entered the house through a tiny window at the back of the house. They had also carefully examined footprints in the soil beneath the window, which indicated that the burglar wore small trainers. They could only conclude that they were looking for a small, slim burglar, identity unknown.

Mr Hopkins was not satisfied. He went to see his golfing friend, the Chief Inspector, who said his force was quite baffled. Then, when the furious man was confronted by his children who complained about Billy Crabtree's thieving ways, his suspicions were aroused. Again he went to see his friend at the police-station. He was assured that Billy Crabtree would be investigated. So, on the morning after the torchlit raid on The Secret Wood, a young constable launched a raid of his own. He made sure he arrived at the Crabtree house one hour before schooltime in order to catch Billy in. He was very apologetic. He could see that Mrs Crabtree was flustered and alarmed by his visit.

'I'm sorry about this, Mrs Crabtree,' he said, accepting a cup of tea. 'But there's been a burglary at Mr Hopkins the solicitor's house, and I need to have a word with Billy.'

'My Billy a burglar, nonsense!' said Mrs Crabtree. 'He may borrow things from time to time, but never to keep. But I'll call him.'

Her nervous cry brought all the children and Buff crowding into the lounge. The young constable took out his notebook and looked stern.

'Now, Billy, where were you last Friday night?'

'I was here watching telly,' said Billy, trying to be brave.

'What were you doing on Friday morning? According to my information, you stole a roller-skate from a certain Miss Valerie Bryant.'

'I did not,' said Billy, indignantly. 'I borrowed the skate from an alsation outside the shops. Anyway, she's got it back.'

'There's also the case of the bicycle, stolen from Cyril Hopkins,' persisted the young man. 'Was that also borrowed?'

'Yes it was,' said Billy. 'And most of the gears didn't work. Joe found it and took it back.'

'Have you ever borrowed valuable coins, Billy?' asked the constable, gently. 'Are you interested in ancient coins?'

'That's enough,' said Mrs Crabtree, sharply. 'Billy is getting ready for school. I won't have him cross-examined when he's got lessons to worry about.'

But the constable was obliged to do his job. 'Have you got any old coins, Billy?'

'Stacks,' said Billy, proudly. 'Gold ones and silver ones and funny-shaped ones.'

'Where did you get them, son?' asked the patient constable. 'Were they borrowed, and where do you keep them?'

'My coins aren't borrowed,' said Billy. He grinned. 'I keep them in a place nobody knows about. I never look at them in case I'm tempted to buy sweets and comics. Because when I've collected enough I'm going to take Mum on a cruise around the world. Dad promised he would some day, now I'm going to do it.'

'What a wonderful thought, Billy,' said his mum, hugging him.

'Billy,' insisted the constable. 'Would these coins be anywhere around the rubbish-dump where you usually leave your borrowed things? I must know the answer, lad.'

'Never there,' chuckled Billy. 'The stuff on the rubbish-dump is meant to be found. But not my coin collection. I'm saving them in my private bank until they mount up to a million pounds. And all it took to find them was pocket-money, saved every week for months.'

'Officer,' interrupted Mrs Crabtree. 'I think you've browbeaten my son long enough. He hasn't had his cornflakes yet.'

'I don't think anyone could browbeat Billy,' smiled the constable. Then he was serious. 'The reason I'm asking these questions is because the house of Mr Hopkins was broken into, and a collection of valuable coins stolen.'

'And the culprit must be our Billy?' said Joe, scornfully. 'He's not perfect, but he'd never break into people's houses. Why are we Crabtrees always blamed when things go wrong or missing?'

'I'm sorry, but I have my job to do,' said the constable, tucking away his notebook. 'Now, having talked to Billy, I can find no evidence that he might have committed a crime. Sometimes I don't like my job, but the law is the law, Mrs Crabtree.'

'Do you know what Mr Micawber said about the law?' challenged Jakey. 'He said the law was an ass. That was when he was waiting for something to turn up. Wait a bit, I'm getting my books mixed up.'

'Or was it the Beadle who said that?' smiled the man. 'Or something like it. We read the same books, young Jakey. But I hope you don't think I'm an ass.'

'I don't,' said Josie, admiring the young man's handsome profile. 'You've done your duty very well, even if you did upset us.'

'I'm glad you've found Billy innocent,' said Jenny. 'And you got to the truth without once hitting him with your truncheon. I'm due to feed the hens before I go to school. Would you like a new-laid egg for your tea?'

'I certainly would,' said the constable. Jenny dashed away. One minute later she returned with a still warm, speckly brown egg.

'Thank you very much,' said the constable, slipping it under his hat.

'If you tell me where you live, we can go to Sunday School together,' said Jenny, laying her plans to marry him when she grew up. 'I can call for you, or you can call for me.'

'I'm sorry, but I'm on duty most Sundays,' he apologised. He rose to leave. Turning at the front door he said. 'Mrs Crabtree, I may need to talk to Billy again, though I hope not. Thanks for the tea and the new-laid egg.'

'Now hop it,' shouted Christie, levelling his dummy like a gun. Buff growled and snapped his teeth. After ruffling Christie's hair and tickling Buff's ear, the nice young constable left.

'What about these coins, Billy?' said Joe, curiously. 'I didn't know you collected coins. And where is this safe place you keep them?'

Billy grinned and tapped the side of his nose. The matter was closed. When Billy had a secret, he was harder to prize open than a clam . . .

Val and Angela arrived at school that day with swollen red legs. The nettles of the previous night had done their work. Cyril had come down with a heavy cold. He spent most of the morning snuffling into a large hanky and dabbing his watering eyes. Suffering so, the three were pleased to hear about the police raid on the Crabtree house. At least their enemies were suffering too.

But the events there didn't please them at all. It appeared that the constable who had stormed the house had cleared Billy of the crime of stealing Mr Hopkins' coin collection and had left the house with a new-laid egg for his tea. Also, according to Jenny, who was shouting it all over the playground, the constable was calling for her on Sunday to take her to Sunday School. And as far as the insults of the previous night were concerned, Joe and Josie Crabtree weren't about to face serious charges.

The three bitterly believed that the Crabtrees had used all their ruffian charm to make the constable side with them. Wincing through their aches and pains, they stared hatefully at Joe and Josie. The Crabtrees reacted in their different ways. Josie stuck out her tongue, while Joe studiously ignored them.

'We are paying attention, I hope,' said the teacher, noticing and frowning. 'I hope I'm not talking to myself?'

Joe was paying attention. The class was discussing the hole in the ozone layer. The teacher sounded worried as she pointed out the alarming blank bits on her map of the Antarctic. Joe felt worried too . . .

Two floors down in the Junior Section Billy was a hero. Many times he was urged to recount how the Flying Squad had smashed down the Crabtree front door at the crack of dawn to catch their suspect unawares.

'I was wanted, you see,' he said, mysteriously.

'For a daring crime I didn't commit. But I had a cast-iron alibi. I was watching the telly at the time the crime took place. I was innocent, but they were determined to get their man. But they didn't . . .'

'Because the law is an ass,' piped Jakey from the crush. 'What's borrowing a skate and a bike got to do with serious crime?'

'Though the arresting officer was very good-looking,' said Jenny. 'I gave the law a new-laid egg for its tea and it's calling again to ask me to marry it.'

Then it was back to the classrooms for more lessons. Though everyone, including the teachers, were glad when the school day ended.

Eight

A THREAT BECOMES REALITY

There had been rumours for some time. Like most places, Chinnbrook Wood fed on rumours and gossip. Usually a rumour faded, to be replaced by another. This one didn't. It flared into life again with the arrival of the men on Wednesday morning. This was a rumour that was about to stick, and become reality.

'I told you,' said the village gossip. 'My husband works for the Council so he should know. They've definitely sold a part of The Dingles to a rich city company who plan to build a supermarket on the site.'

It seemed to be true. Shoppers in the High Street could see for themselves the workmen in their luminous orange jackets, and others in sharp suits walking about jotting notes on their clipboards. One or two carried small telescopes on tripods and long red-and-white poles. Most ominous of all was the arrival of a bright yellow bulldozer that advanced towards the trees and bushes, its jaws menacingly raised.

The news reached the school about midday. First there was shock, then bewilderment and anger. The treachery of the Council defied belief. How dare they act in such an undercover way! The Dingles belonged to children, not to rich men sitting in offices! Everything was disrupted as children from both sides of the bridge expressed their rage. The grapevine news continued to filter in. It seemed the company intended to demolish the old stone bridge and divert the Chinnbrook stream in order to make room for their supermarket and car-park.

'And where do you think they plan to build their huge horror?' discussed the enraged children. 'Only where The Secret Wood is, that's where!'

'They're going to chop and bulldoze the wood down,' said Joe to Josie, both angry and sad. 'All the animals and birds and plants will be swept away so that they can lay it over with concrete and paving-stones, and plants in tubs.'

'Oh, the lovely yellow-hammers,' wept Josie on his shoulder. 'Concreted out of existence.'

'There must be *something* we can do,' said Joe, suddenly defiant. Then he shrugged his shoulders. 'But what?'

In another part of the school grounds a similar conversation was taking place.

'The cheek!' stormed Val. 'How dare this uncaring Company chop down The Secret Wood when I haven't completed my article about Queen Gertie? Cyril, your dad is still a solicitor, even though he botched up the thieving Billy Crabtree case. Couldn't he tackle the Company's plans and put a spoke in their works? In that way he might regain our respect again. And after all, the Company would be a lot easier to beat than Billy Crabtree.'

'This morning when he got in his car he shouted he was fed-up trying to sort out the problems of children,' said Angela, shame-faced. 'He said he had more important business to worry about, and that we should sort out our own problems.'

'Well, that's told us,' grimaced Val. 'And my dad's only a bank manager, so he's no use.'

'Oh, the poor Dingles,' said Angela, sadly. 'And

our half of the old stone bridge. 'There must be something we can do.'

'I know,' agreed Val. 'It breaks my heart to think of them chopping down Queen Gertie's cherry-tree with her golden rolling-pin inside. Now I'll never learn the history of that sad lady.'

'If only we could fight these powerful people,' said Cyril. 'But we haven't many good fighters on our side of the bridge.'

'There are plenty of good fighters on the Crabtree side,' said Val, thoughtfully. 'I wonder . . .'

'You're not thinking what I think you're thinking?' said Angela, aghast.

'I'll talk to mum while she's peeling the potatoes this afternoon,' said Val. 'She says amazingly wise things while she's peeling potatoes.'

'So, by tomorrow morning we should have a plan,' said Cyril.

'Let's hope so,' Val replied. 'Come on, we can talk on the way home.'

Slinging their school-bags over their shoulders, they joined the stream of other children wending their way home . . .

'Well, it's quite clear, dear,' said Mrs Bryant, plopping another potato into the saucepan. She was making a cottage-pie for dinner. 'You and your friends must stop feuding with the Crabtrees and get together over this. Though I doubt if all the demonstrations in the world will budge a powerful company. But I agree with you, it's sheer vandalism to plan to destroy The Dingles. I remember my own happy days playing there.'

'But will the Crabtrees talk to us?' said Val. 'Especially after the big fight we had on the bridge?'

'What do you think, Bob?' said Mrs Bryant. 'You know Joe Crabtree. Do you think he'll be making plans of his own to save The Secret Wood? Do you think he'd be ready to join forces with Val and her friends?'

'Well,' said Bob, his huge trainers propped up on the kitchen-table. 'I'm not into trees and bushes myself. A concrete hard-rock jungle is more my scene. But if you're asking me, I'd say Val would have to crawl on her bended knees before Joe came around. He's a good guy, but he's astonishingly proud. But, as I say, I'm not into vegetation.'

'Crawl on my knees to Joe Crabtree?' cried Val. 'I'd rather die!'

'Or allow The Secret Wood to die,' said her mum, quietly. 'You must swallow that false pride of yours and meet the Crabtrees half-way.'

'Like you did on the bridge,' grinned Bob. 'Though it's all a mystery to me. The world is full of other bushes and trees, so what's all the fuss about? But then life's full of mystery, they say . . .'

'Here, work out the mystery in that,' said his mother, tossing him a Spanish onion. 'And if you can't understand it, peel it. And Valerie, you can mash the potatoes when they're cooked, seeing that you've set up home in my kitchen.'

'I'll think about what you've said, mum,' said Val. 'About making peace with Joe Crabtree.'

'You do that,' was the reply. 'And don't take too long about it!'

'I'm not surprised,' said Mrs Crabtree. 'The Council and the money-men must have been plotting this for ages. They'll bulldoze down anything if there's a profit to be made.'

'Money is the root of all evil,' said Jakey, gravely. 'Mr Micawber often said that, when he was broke.'

'What can we do against powerful men,' said Josie, shaking her red curls. 'It's no good appealing to their better nature because they haven't got one. What could we say if we confronted them?'

'Hop it!' shouted Christie. Buff barked, though he was more in the dark than his little master. 'Joe,' appealed Josie. 'Stop sitting with your head in your hands like a poet and rap out a plan. Your yellow-hammers won't stand a chance when the bulldozers roar in. If we don't fight then we'll regret it for the rest of our lives.'

'This Valerie Bryant,' said their mum, curiously. 'She and her friends seem to care about The Dingles as much as you. Why not join forces and fight your enemies together?'

'Team up with Valerie Bryant and the Hopkins? No thanks!' said Joe.

'They're real snobs,' agreed Josie. 'And they'd be useless in a fight.'

'I wouldn't mind being a snob if I had the latest

bike every year like Cyril,' said Billy, wistfully. 'It isn't the same just having one ride when you know it has to go back. I expect Cyril will have the latest powerful motorbike when he gets older, while I'll just have to borrow a ride on it.'

'Who's for chips and mushy peas and fish-fingers?' interrupted their mum, doling out the portions. She smiled. 'I do believe this is the first time I've seen that television blank. So, if the Cause of The Secret Wood means so much to you, start planning what to do. And while you're planning, don't forget to open a tin for Buff, and to feed the cat and the goldfish. And Jenny, don't forget the scraps for the hens. I'm going round to Susie's now. It's our Bingo night. Don't forget to put the young ones to bed, Josie. And if you must play pop-music, play it softly – we have neighbours.'

'I'll think about what you said, mum,' said Joe.

'I'm glad to hear it,' she replied. 'This nonsense between you and that girl has gone on long enough.'

She slipped on her coat and left.

The telly remained off, which was quite extra-ordinary. The Crabtree children had important things to discuss.

'Organisation, that's what we need,' said Joe. 'There are lots of kids who think as we do about The Dingles. At least we can put up a fight against the bulldozers and the chain-saw men.'

'Banners,' said Billy. 'What we need are lots of bright banners with insulting messages on them. Like – "The Council and the Company men are a herd of fascist pigs . . .". Something biting like that. I can borrow the stuff we'll need from school.'

'There'll be no borrowing involved, Billy,' said Josie, sternly. 'You can visit your rubbish-dump and bring home some old cardboard boxes to write on. Jakey and Christie can be in charge of crayoning the protests, Jakey being gifted with words and Christie owning the crayon-box. Jenny, who is a dab-hand with a hammer and nails, she having built the henhouse on her own, can hammer the slogans on to sticks.'

'Now we're getting somewhere,' said Joe, pleased. He looked thoughtful. 'What we need is a powerful slogan to launch our cause . . .'

'Hop it,' shouted Christie, rummaging in his toy-box for his crayon-set, Buff pushing his wet nose inside to help.

Everyone laughed. Then it was back to serious matters. They were still making plans when Mrs Crabtree returned home from her night out . . .

Nine

A WARY TRUCE

It was Val who made the first move. At lunchtime in school the next day she actually smiled at Joe – which made him nervous. Then Angela grinned, while Cyril gave him a friendly thumbs-up sign. This unnerved him even more. Josie, noticing, shrewdly realised that the sudden friendliness was leading up to something. It could only mean that their enemies were sucking up to Joe in order to play a role in the saving of The Dingles. Which could be useful even though you disliked your allies. Allies, even snooty ones from across the bridge were desperately needed. So when Val turned her smile on her, Josie smiled bleakly back. She was anxious to talk to her brother. To her dismay she saw that Joe had already been cornered by a hair-tossing Val, all smiles and fluttering lashes . . .

'Don't you think we should stop being nasty to each other and be friends?' said Val, coming straight to the point. 'After all, we both love The Dingles and The Secret Wood. I know we love The Secret Wood for different reasons, but can't we join forces to save the land we love from the bulldozers?'

'It's a thought,' said Joe, coolly. 'But me and my family have already got a plan we're working on. I'm not sure we need any more volunteers. Though I'm prepared to listen to anyone who wants to save The Dingles.'

'Then listen to me, Joe,' said Val, smiling with relief. 'This morning in class I had an idea that might help . . .'

Which was quite untrue. She had been thinking and plotting all through the previous day and night. She had taken up Bob's suggestion that she should invite Joe to the pictures and a coke in the cafe afterwards. The problem was that the film showing at the Odeon was a violent American action movie, and she guessed Joe wouldn't like that, he being a sensitive poet. So before school she had nipped into the video-shop. The video she had rented was in her school-bag.

Carefully timing the moment she made the boy an offer he could not politely refuse, 'Why don't we discuss my idea, Joe?' she said. 'Why don't you come to our house after tea? We could watch my favourite video. It's a two-hour tape of Sir John Betjeman, full of lovely poems and church towers. Would you like to see it? I know you like poetry. Please don't say no because my mum is dying to meet you properly.'

'I don't know, I'll probably be busy planning tactics with my family tonight,' he said. But he was pleased, which explained the blush on his face. He was noting how different this girl was when she wasn't pouting and sulking. It was the first time he had really been close to her and he was intrigued to see that her eyes were the colour of yellow-hammer eggs.

'Please say yes,' she appealed. 'I don't want us to be enemies any more. And my mum just adores your hedgehog poem.'

'Well, I suppose I can spare a couple of hours,' said Joe, flattered.

'Three hours,' said Val, quickly. 'Two for the

John Betjeman video and an hour for talking afterwards. About the saving of The Secret Wood. Shall we say six o'clock, prompt?'

'Okay,' said Joe, casually. But he was glowing inside and out.

After she'd left to join Angela and Cyril, Josie finally cornered him. Suspiciously she listened as he explained about Val's invitation.

'You know what her game is, Joe,' she warned. 'She wants to save The Secret Wood for her own selfish reasons, and she's using you to do it. Did she once mention the saving of yellow-hammers? I doubt it. Go along if you must, but don't be taken in by her wily charms.'

'As if I would be,' scoffed Joe. 'I'm just curious to know what she's got to say. And stop looking at me like that and smile. That's better . . .'

They were both smiling as they walked back to the classroom to tackle another session of algebra. Throughout the lesson Val and Angela and Cyril continued to smile at Joe each time they caught his eye. They didn't smile much at Josie, because she was an expert at pulling hideous faces. For the rest of the school-day Joe felt a bit like a mouse being hypnotised by the gaze of three, too-friendly snakes . . .

'One pair of clean jeans, Joe,' said Mrs Crabtree, handing them to her son.

'One tee-shirt, daz-white and ironed,' giggled Jenny, throwing it at him. 'And your trainers all spruced to perfection,' smiled Josie, showing them.

Embarrassed, Joe went into the kitchen to change. He returned.

'You look just like Pip from *Great Expectations*,' said Jakey. 'He was always poshing up to impress a girl who looked down her nose at him.'

'Take no notice, Joe,' said Mrs Crabtree. 'You look very handsome. Now go and be a credit to us.'

'See you, then,' said Joe, pausing at the front door and trying to ignore the sniggers.

'Hop it!' yelled Christie, puffing on his dummy. Buff crouched beside him wagging his smelly stump of a tail.

'Just don't get engaged on the first date, that's

all,' smiled Josie as her brother slammed the front door behind him.

Then for Mrs Crabtree and her family it was time to settle back and watch the unlikely love-affairs on the Australian soaps. They had no worries about their son and brother. He wouldn't get himself into a silly love-tangle. Joe could take care of himself. And he would return as familar as ever with a friendly clip on the ear for the young ones, plus a goodnight story and kiss for each . . .

'Don't fuss, Mum,' said Val, crossly. 'It's only Joe Crabtree after all. And when he comes, don't gush about his poems.'

'"The Hedgehog" was a lovely poem,' said Mrs Bryant, defensively.

'What time is your Lord Byron coming?' asked Bob. He was sitting on top of the fridge tuning his guitar.

'Six o'clock, and you can shut up,' snapped Val.

'Are all those cress and tuna sandwiches just for you two?' asked Bob, astonished. 'You'll never put that lot away. Can I come in the front room later and . . ?'

'You dare,' warned Val, slapping his hand away from the tray.

'Shall I let him in when the doorbell rings, Val?' said Mrs Bryant. 'After all, I am the lady of this house . . .'

Just at that moment the bell rang. It was smack on the stroke of six. Mrs Bryant hurried to open it.

'Good evening, Joe,' said the lady. 'I was just reading your poem again and I think it's wonderful.'

'Mother,' called Val from the kitchen. 'Dad's steak is over-grilling and his onions are turning black.'

'Oh goodness, excuse me, Joe,' said Mrs Bryant, rushing away. Val replaced her at the door and ushered Joe into the front room. After a friendly 'Thanks for coming' she sat him down and clicked on the video-machine. During the next two hours Joe saw so many gothic arches and heard so many poems about the seaside that his head began to spin. Though he did enjoy the cress and tuna sandwiches. At long last the video was over.

'Now for our vital talk, Joe,' said Val. 'About the danger to The Dingles and The Secret Wood. I'll now explain my great idea. What if we put aside our separate articles for the school magazine and wrote one together? About the Company men's plans to destroy everything with their supermarket? I could tell the historical story about Queen Gertie, and you could mention your yellow-hammers. If we wrote it full of punch we'd have everyone on our side, I'm sure, even the telly and newspapers.'

'Me and Josie have our own plans,' said Joe, warily. 'We're making banners and planning a protest.'

'My dad is a bank manager,' Val persisted. 'He knows lots of important people who could help our cause. And Angela and Cyril's dad is a clever solicitor who knows how to slip through the loopholes in the law. Don't forget, Joe, we'll need all the help we can get. When we fight we're going to need powerful people behind us.'

'It's powerful people who want to destroy the countryside,' said Joe, cynically. 'Me and my family don't want their likes butting in. When we fight for the wood we'll do it without the help of grown-ups who can't understand.'

'You said "we", Joe,' said Val, beaming. 'Which must mean I'm included. So we *are* going to join forces. I intend to start my part of the article tonight.'

'I didn't mean "we" like that,' said Joe, hastily. 'I need time to think about it . . .' Just then the door burst open and Bob slouched into the room. He slumped into an armchair.

'How's it going, Joe?' he asked. 'I see you couldn't manage all the sandwiches,' and he began to stuff down what remained on the tray.

'Guess what,' said Val, happily. 'Me and Joe are forming The Committee For The Saving of The Dingles and The Secret Wood, aren't we Joe?'

'I don't know about a committee,' said Joe, confused. He knew Val was overbearing, but this was a bit too much. 'Me and Josie and the others never thought about a committee. We just planned to make some placards to demonstrate, and send a letter of protest to our Member of Parliament.'

Bob shook his head. 'A waste of time. What you need is a head-on fight and plenty of bruises to show, to get noticed. Politicians are hopeless when it comes to action. And a good idea would be to phone the Green Party and ask if they've got a spare folk-group to strum and sing about the destruction of nature. If you're aggressive you'll get on T.V. and plenty of press coverage, which is what you need. Only suggestions, mind, it's your committee after all.'

'Yes, it is,' snapped Val. 'Will you please mind your own business.'

'I didn't know there was a committee,' said Joe, bewildered. 'I haven't mentioned one.'

'Anyway,' said Bob, yawning and rising. 'Listening to twittering yellow-hammers and watching flowers grow isn't my idea of fun. Nor grubbing about for a golden rolling-pin which doesn't exist. But all the best, Joe, see you . . .' and he ambled out of the room.

'Now, I think we should draw up a list of our forces,' said Val, excitedly. 'There's me and

Angela and Cyril, and you and Josie and a few others . . .'

'Hold on,' said Joe, fed-up. 'It's my plan, yet you seem to be taking charge!'

Val smiled sweetly. 'Then you take charge, Joe. I'll gladly serve as your humble follower.'

'I don't know,' Joe hesitated. 'I'll have to talk to Josie.'

'Of course,' said Val. 'And when you've gone I'll phone Angela and Cyril to come round. I can't wait to start making plans for The Battle Of The Weekend.'

'What Battle Of The Weekend?' said Joe, astonished.

'The battle the committee is going to wage against the Company and the bulldozers on Saturday,' replied Val, impatiently. 'Now I expect you're anxious to get home to talk things over with Josie. Would you like to borrow my bike? You'll be home a lot sooner.'

'No thanks,' said Joe, weakly. 'I've always liked walking.'

Then Val sprang the trap she had been plotting for the last three hours. 'Oh, by the way, as officials of the committee, me and my friends will need to have free access to your side of the bridge. But that's enough for now, Joe. I see you're anxious to get home so I'll see you out. Are you sure you don't want to borrow my bike . . . ?' and she led him into the hall.

Mrs Bryant had hurried from the back room where she and her tired husband liked to listen to their old Beatles records for relaxation. She had heard the movement in the hall.

'I hope you've had a nice evening, Joe. Have you two got everything sorted out?' She wagged a finger. 'And don't neglect your poetry. The next time you come I hope to be reading another of your lovely verses. Goodnight.'

'Goodnight, Joe,' said Val, flashing him a lovely smile. 'I've enjoyed our evening very much.'

'Goodnight, and thank you,' said Joe in a daze.

Walking down the quiet road through the late summer mist Joe could have kicked himself. Valerie Bryant had wound him round her finger and he had been helpless to prevent it. A car raced down the road towards him, its headlights glaring. For a moment he was mesmerised by the dazzle. The thought occurred that countless small animals had been trapped in such situations, not knowing which way to flee. Just like he at Valerie Bryant's house. However, things would be different when he was back on familiar ground – at home. Though he had to admit to a sneaking admiration for the cunning way Val had outwitted him. And her eyes were ever and always the colour of yellow-hammer eggs . . . and then he was home . . .

'She said what?' said Josie, angrily. 'Honestly, Joe Crabtree, you're as soft as butter. Trying to take over our protest . . . the nerve! Well, I'll be having a word with her in the morning. Nobody treats my brother like that!'

Ignoring his protests, she packed him off to bed, for Josie was very strong-willed. Joe was grateful to go.

The owl hooted outside the window as if mocking and chiding the boy. But the boy was fast asleep . . .

Ten

EMERGENCY ACTION STATIONS

On their way to school Joe tried to curb Josie's anger, but to no avail. The girl was determined to have it out face-to-face with Valerie Bryant. While Joe walked miserably down the school drive, Josie planted herself outside the gates and waited for the usually late Valerie to arrive with her friends. She kept her anger bright by thinking about her brother's treatment the previous night. Just then, Billy came racing along the pavement. As usual he had paid one of his mysterious visits to the village rubbish-dump before coming to school.

'The bulldozer has started up and it's advancing on The Secret Wood!' he gasped to Josie. 'We'd better be quick if we're going to save the trees.'

'Run into school and tell Joe,' Josie ordered. She took to her heels in the direction of The Dingles.

The teachers were astonished and annoyed

when Billy burst through the swing-doors and began to shout into the classrooms that the Company bulldozers were stealing a march on them. Seconds later, a mass truancy began, Joe and Val in the lead. The horde of angry children arrived at The Dingles to see Josie lying in front of a bulldozer shouting rude words at the driver. A small knot of annoyed men were trying to persuade her to move out of the way. While Joe and Val and Angela and Cyril marched forward to support Josie, Billy shinned up a tree on the edge of The Secret Wood and strapped himself to the highest branch with an old bit of rope he had found.

'What school do you children come from?' demanded an angry man in a smart suit, waving his clipboard. 'And why aren't you there? This site is private property and you're holding up work.'

'Never mind about our schooling,' said Joe, advancing fearlessly. 'And don't talk to us about private property. We're here to defend The Secret Wood and the old stone bridge that has always belonged to us. We don't need to prove our claim with millions of pounds, for it's ours because its always been so. It's also the property of the sacred yellow-hammers by birthright.'

'And the ancient cherry-tree belongs to history because of Queen Gertie,' yelled Val. 'So move your horrible machine off our heritage.'

'You refuse to move then?' said the furious man to the children. 'I can always call the police.'

'I hope he calls my special constable with the blue eyes,' said Jenny, dreamily.

'Are you going back to school, or not?' shouted the angry man. For answer, a half-dozen children flung themselves to join Josie in front of the huge tyres of the bulldozer, not caring that they muddied their school uniforms. Val joined them, flinging herself into the mud beside Josie.

The man spoke into his mobile-phone for some time. It was obvious he was having arguments, for his face was bright-red. Then he spoke again.

'I've called the police and your Headmaster is on his way here,' he shouted.

'It's no good sending for the law,' said Jakey, shaking his head. 'They're all in the cafes scoffing bacon-butties. They refuse to arrest anybody until

they've had a good breakfast. As for our Head-master, he's no Mr Squeers from *Nicholas Nickleby*, he's much too kind. He'll never lock us up and feed us gruel.'

'Anyway,' said Cyril. 'Our teachers are glad to see the back of us. They're always saying we aren't worth teaching.'

'If you won't go back to school, then you leave me no choice,' said the man, grimly. He dialled another number on his phone and spoke urgently, watched by the now hushed crush of children. They knew it was too late to go back on their determination. But the battle had been joined and they knew it must be stuck out to the end.

Quite soon, a police-car juddered up the track. Out of it stepped a familiar constable, much to Jenny's delight.

'Did you enjoy your egg for your tea?' she called. She was disappointed when he didn't reply. He looked stern as he spoke to the man with the clip-board. Then he turned to the gaggle of children.

'I am ordering you to go back to school,' he said. He bent down and spoke to Josie and Val and the others who lay stubbornly before the wheels of the bulldozer. 'And I mean all of you.'

'Never,' cried Josie. 'We're not leaving until this bulldozer does.'

'You'll have to saw me in half before you get me out of this tree,' shouted Billy from high up. 'Then you'll be in trouble when my mum finds out.'

The policeman was speaking into his own phone. After much nodding and a few 'yes, sirs', he addressed the man with the clipboard and the children. He looked grave and anxious. 'My Inspector is on his way and so is your school Headmaster. I'm ordering you to behave yourselves when they arrive, or I might be making handcuffed arrests. In the meantime I've told the bulldozer to switch off its engine. As the law, I'm in charge here until my Inspector arrives.'

To loud cheers Josie and Val and their supporters hauled themselves from the mud and tried to brush their uniforms clean. The driver of the switched-off bulldozer sat in his cab and munched his sandwiches while studying the racing form in his newspaper. He took little notice of the protest banners waving round his windows. He had seen it all before.

The Chief Inspector arrived amid a squeal of brakes, a blue light flashing on his car. At the same time the Headmaster came wobbling up the track on his bicycle. The men gathered together and spoke awhile against the background hum of the angry children. Presently the Inspector stepped forward and addressed them.

'It is agreed that the cutting down of the trees will not start today,' he said. 'Mr Grimes, the site-manager, is stopping all work while he consults with his Company office. However, the proper place for you children is in school. A moral for you all. I never missed a day from school and look where it got me. I will now hand over to your Headmaster who will no doubt deal severely with your ring-leaders,' and away he sped in his power-ful car with the constable trailing behind in his modest one. He ignored Jakey's curled-lip sneer.

'I don't need to tell you I'm very angry,' said the Headmaster to the subdued children. He glanced behind and up. 'And you can come down from the tree, Billy Crabtree.'

'Won't!' shouted Billy, defiantly. 'I intend to build a stronghold up here. I know where I can borrow the ropes and wood from.'

The Headmaster shook his head and turned back to the others. 'I agree that the saving of the countryside is very important. But it won't be achieved by you leaving your place of learning and running amok. Now, though you are not nursery children, nevertheless I'm going to treat you as such. As punishment for your behaviour, you will form a crocodile formation and follow me back to school. If you think it is shaming, then it will teach you never to leave school without permission again. Ah, I see Billy has joined us. Right, form up and follow me . . .'

Walking his bike before them, the Headmaster led the humiliated children back to school to the amusement of the hardened truants who hooted as they passed by. Yet Joe and Josie and Val felt pride that they had fought off the first Company attack. Back in class they found learning very dull after the excitement of the morning. Meanwhile they had to content themselves with rumours that came through the grapevine. They were relieved to hear that the bulldozer remained switched off and its driver had gone home for his tea.

As they studied in the quiet of the classroom, Josie was reflecting. She was beginning to feel admiration and respect for Val and her friends. She remembered how the three had stood firmly beside her and Joe, or in Val's case, lay. Josie turned in her seat and smiled at her once bitter enemies. The once bitter enemies smiled back. A friendship was developing, an age-old bridge of hostility was beginning to crumble.

The bulldozer stood cold and silent for that day and through the night. Through Friday it still slumped before the trees of The Secret Wood, looking like a huge yellow dinosaur that didn't know what to do. While it lay inert and unable to challenge them, Billy and a couple of close friends were busying themselves in the highest tree at the edge of the wood. With the aid of a rickety rope-ladder, things, were being hauled aloft . . .

Saturday came, as did the morning paper . . .

Eleven

BLACK SATURDAY

SCHOOL CHILDREN DEFY BIG BUSINESS COMPANY. Plans to demolish an old stone bridge and parts of the ancient Dingles to build a super-market on the site were frustrated by the children from a local school who flung themselves in front of the bulldozers. 'Our workers will go in,' promised the chairman of the company. 'Oh no they won't,' say the kids. According to our information, Saturday will be the big crunch day.

'Eat your breakfast,' scolded Mrs Bryant. 'You can't fight bulldozers on an empty stomach.'

Val ignored her and dashed up the stairs to gather the equipment she would need for a long siege. Bob shook his head as he came down the stairs. He had been woken by Val stuffing his one-man tent into her haversack.

'You can't fight big money, Mum,' he said, eating his own and Val's breakfast. 'That's why I intend to become enormously rich when me and my band tour the world. Then I'll be a fat cat in my own right.'

'Lovely, dear,' said his mum. She jumped as Val barged into the kitchen. She was shouldering a huge burden of stuff.

'If I'm not home for tea, phone the police-station,' she said. 'I'll probably be locked up in a cell on bread-and-water . . .' and she staggered out to meet up with Angela and Cyril.

'Impulsive girl,' murmured Mrs Bryant. 'Your father is thinking of putting his foot down.'

'He tried it with me, but it was no use,' said Bob. 'How could I work in a bank with all this rock-and-roll inside me?'

'And you'd have to wear your hair much shorter in a bank,' agreed his mum. 'But I wish Valerie didn't throw herself into her enthusiasms so totally. I hope her pranks don't appear on *Midlands News*. Your father is trying to digest his dinner about then.'

'She's hungry for publicity,' said Bob, wisely.

'But when you've had enough of it you bury yourself like a hermit in the south of France, in a villa by the sea. I intend to shun all publicity when I make it big.'

'That's sensible, dear,' said Mrs Bryant. She turned and raised her skillet. 'Now, will you be wanting more eggs and bacon? Or perhaps frogs-legs and snails to get you used to your new life in France . . . ?'

Val and Angela and Cyril stumbled along the misty path through The Dingles. But their stumbling was lighter than on previous times. They could now cross the old stone bridge to the Crabtree side united against a common enemy, the Company. As usual, Cyril was carrying the latest inventions from America. These included a Utility-Belt stuffed with amazing gadgets guaranteed to save your life in emergencies. The advert had read that Batman would never be without one. Sadly, even his high-tech stuff couldn't prevent him from toppling into the same toad-pond he had toppled into before.

They were dismayed by the sight that greeted

them when they emerged from the trees on to the bridge. On the Crabtree side hulked another orange monster with a huge metal ball swinging on the end of a cable. One glance could tell that it was designed to destroy things. Its engine throbbed throatily as the man in the cab waited for the order to knock something to bits. Behind the machine were a few men with PRIVATE SECURITY printed on their orange jackets. Standing close beside were two police constables sent to keep order. But the most astonishing sight was at the centre of the bridge. Chained to its metal safety-rail were Joe and Josie, cheered on by early-bird kids from both sides of the bridge. They were waving placards and chanting,

'LEAVE IT ALONE. THIS BRIDGE IS OUR OWN. IT'S NOTHING TO DO WITH YOU . . . !'

Cyril shrugged out of his arctic rucksack and raced to join the brave ones on the bridge. With an agility that belied his stoutness, he leapt upwards to straddle the gently swinging ball. The driver in the cab took not the slightest notice. He was being paid, so why should he care? Presently the Chief Inspector from yesterday arrived, amid squealing brakes again. He advanced and addressed the rebels through a loud-hailer.

'You are breaking the law,' he boomed. 'I'm ordering you to stop this nonsense and go home.'

'We'll go home after you order the Company men to leave The Dingles alone,' yelled Joe from his chains. 'And not a second before.'

'And be warned,' shouted Josie. 'Touch one hair of our heads and you'll be sued for child abuse. Just tell them to take that horrible machine away.'

Then she saw Val and Angela standing on the bridge itching for something to do to help the cause. She cried, 'Run to The Secret Wood and help Billy and his friends. They are bravely defying the men with the tree-cutting saws. Don't worry about us – we'll hold out . . .'

Previously, in secret, Billy and his helpers had borrowed enough materials to build a strong fortress in the high tree. With a stock of crisps and coke and their Walkmans to fill the lonely hours, they believed they could hold out for ever, even if ever was a very long time.

As Val and Angela arrived, all out of breath,

so did the newsmen and the clicking photographers.

'Hang in there, Billy,' Val shouted up into the thick branches. 'We've just left Joe and Josie chained to the bridge and Cyril clinging to a metal ball, but they're quite alright.'

'Okay up here,' Billy shouted back. 'But we need some Mars-bars and *The Lord Of The Rings*. We need something long to read. And a strong torch with spare batteries in case we need to read till Christmas.'

'Just hang in there, Billy and Co,' called Angela. 'Your requests will be delivered as soon as possible. I haven't got *The Lord Of The Rings* in my bookcase, but I do have *Budgie The Little Helicopter*. Will that do?'

There was a long silence from the branches above. Then Billy shouted. 'Just don't forget the Mars-bars.'

'Request understood, Billy,' yelled Val. 'Don't worry, my brother Bob has got a copy of *The Lord Of The Rings*. Me and Angela are now going to have a few sharp words with the driver of the bulldozer and the chainsaw men . . .'

'Val,' hissed Angela, excitedly. 'Don't look now, but here comes a reporter and his photographer. I hope they don't snap me full-frontal with mud all over my face. I'll die seeing myself in the news looking like this!'

'Little girls,' asked the reporter. 'Don't you think that you are fighting a lost cause? Big business always wins, everyone knows that.'

'First of all, we are not little girls,' said Val, firmly. 'And secondly, we believe the Company is going to suffer a crushing defeat. And don't smirk as you scribble. I'm a journalist in my own right with lots of articles in the school magazine behind me.'

'And when you take my picture I demand that you snap my left side,' said Angela, posing for the photographer. 'Because I've got spots on the right side of my nose.'

'You're all determined to hold out, then?' said the reporter, mildly impressed. 'You won't give up the fight, no matter what?'

'Never,' said Val, angrily. 'If you want to see real action, hurry down to the old stone bridge where our other combat group are holding out . . .'

and she and Angela hared back to the beleaguered bridge, their mission accomplished here.

'Billy,' the reporter called up the tree, his photographer snapping away. 'How long do you think you can hold out up there?'

'As long as it takes to read *The Lord Of The Rings*, if necessary,' retorted Billy. 'Or until our Mars-bars and coke run out.'

The reporter and his camera friend exchanged grins. Then they looked to where, a few yards away, the chainsaw men and the bulldozer driver were sitting on the grass exchanging sandwiches and opinions. The photographer took a snap of that peaceful scene before loping off with his partner through the tiger-grass to see what was happening at the old stone bridge.

'Billy and Co,' shouted the fed-up bulldozer driver. 'Come down from that tree and I'll give you a ride on my orange dinosaur.'

'When I want to ride an orange dinosaur I'll borrow one,' yelled Billy back. 'Just get on with your picnic and stop trying to tempt us down.'

The battle for the bridge was not going well for the defenders. Just arrived, Val and Angela were dismayed to see that the enemy were winning. Joe and Josie and Cyril had valiantly held out for one full morning. Now they were being overwhelmed by superior forces and equipment. The girls were in time to see a security man snipping through Joe and Josie's chains, and Jenny's adored constable placing them under arrest. Cyril was faring no better. The site-boss had ordered the bulldozer driver to wobble his heavy metal ball. Cyril had clung on bravely, but his queasy stomach let him down. Groggy and pale he was helped down from his perch by the security men.

'Right,' shouted the site-boss to the bulldozer driver. 'Get to work and let's get this bridge smashed down.'

The driver revved his engine to a chorus of jeers from the disappointed kids. He was just about to swing his crushing ball against the stones of the bridge when a Rolls Royce car came speeding up. Cyril and Angela cheered. They knew their dad would never let them down. Mr Hopkins stepped out wearing his solicitor's pinstripes and carrying a heavy briefcase. He had a passenger. Out climbed his golfing friend, the Chief Inspector, his peaked cap gleaming with silver, his little cane under his arm. The Inspector pointed his cane at the bulldozer driver.

'Please switch off your engine. Mr Hopkins the solicitor has something important to say.'

Mr Hopkins approached the bewildered site-boss and flourished a piece of paper. In his best courtroom voice he said, 'I have here a restraining order from a magistrate. It says that all work on this site must cease, pending further investigation. He has ordered a stay of forty-eight hours until the legal problems are sorted out. I have here another document, signed by the Clerk Of The Council. He has agreed to allow me to search through the old files concerning this land. There are some who believe that there might be ancient title-rights gathering dust in the vaults of the Record Office. Very suspicious. As a solicitor I'm beginning to smell a rat . . .'

'Now that's the way to drive a coach-and-horses through the rules,' said Jakey to Cyril. 'Make the law look like an ass and you're home and dry.

Your dad is a real ferret as far as loopholes are concerned.'

'That's why he's rich,' said Cyril, proudly. 'That's why me and Angela always get the latest gadgets and bikes every year.'

'He always pulls out all the stops when me and Cyril are in trouble,' explained Angela. 'He becomes a lion when his cubs are in danger; he always roars to Mum. He loves David whats-his-name's wildlife programmes.'

'So, gentlemen,' said the Inspector to the site-boss and his men. 'You may as well go home while the archives are being dusted off and examined. In the meantime your Company will be kept informed . . .' and he and Mr Hopkins swept away in the Rolls Royce to play a round of golf.

'The Company won't like this,' said the worried site-boss. 'They've invested millions of pounds in this project.'

'Don't worry so,' comforted Val. 'It isn't your fault. They should have done their research more carefully. Now Mr Hopkins has won The Dingles a stay of execution, you and your men can go home to your families. I'm sure none of you will get the sack, because it's all the fault of the Company men.'

The site-boss and his security men departed to await further orders. Muddy and tired, but satisfied, Val and Angela and Cyril said goodbye to their friends the Crabtrees and turned to go home by way of a long enjoyable stroll along the narrow paths of The Dingles, and through the thick tiger-grass . . .

Billy and his friends heard on the grapevine about Mr Hopkins' restraining order. Billy's pals swarmed down the rope-ladder they had fashioned to complete the stronghold in the tree, promising to return if needed. Made of sterner stuff, Billy decided to stay put. He didn't trust solicitors and scraps of legal paper. He trusted his own instincts. He also had an important interest in the saving of The Secret Wood, but he kept that to himself. His adored mum would learn soon enough, when the time was right. In truth he was enjoying his stay in the tree-house. Up here was a gently swaying world where a boy could daydream about tigers prowling through the tiger-grass and about a brand-new bike he didn't have to borrow. Billy was content. And he had the promise of a supply of Mars-bars and a copy of *The Lord Of The Rings*, plus a strong torch to read it by. These things were all he needed to hold out against the powers that threatened to destroy so many dreams . . . Then he heard voices calling upwards.

'Billy,' shouted Joe. 'Come down and come home. We're safe until Monday.'

'It's your favourite bangers and mash for tea,' tempted Josie.

But Billy's stubborn mind was made up. He pushed the mouth-watering image of bangers-and-mash from his mind and began to chew into a bag of salted peanuts, brushing aside the squirrels who were gathering in the tree, who loved them more than he.

'I'll come down when the war is won,' he shouted down. 'Not just one battle but the whole war.'

'So much for Billy,' said Joe to Josie as they made their way home. 'Up a tree and happy, another private little world snug around him.'

'But without nourishment,' said Josie, worried.

The Lord Of The Rings will provide,' smiled Joe. 'And Val's Mars-bars . . .'

'It's a wonderful thing,' said Mrs Crabtree. 'Not only have you won the first round against the money-people, but you've made friends with the children from the other side of the bridge.'

Proudly patting each one of them on the head, she doled out the bangers and mash. Through habit, she served up Billy's extra-large portion. Then, sadly realising he was up a tree she patted the whining Buff and put Billy's plate on the floor for their pet to gobble down. And Buff enjoyed it very much, with ice-cream for afters . . .

Mr Hopkins had not been idle. While playing golf with the Inspector, they caught up with the Clerk Of The Council, as Mr Hopkins guessed they would. The Clerk was in mid-swing when the solicitor approached and whispered in his ear. The Clerk nodded. After the game and a drink at the bar, the pair departed for the Council Records

Office. They remained there for the rest of the day and part of the night, coughing and sneezing from the disturbed dust amongst the piles of ancient, yellowing documents . . .

Twelve

NAIL-BITING SUNDAY

There was much delight on both sides of the bridge when the local Sunday paper ran the story of the children's fight against the rich men for possession of The Dingles. There was a colour picture too. An image of a camouflaged-faced Billy peering down from his tree-house. In bold type the article read . .

WAR IS DECLARED

A large business company has been challenged by school-kids. The company plan to build a supermarket on the site of a local beauty spot. Their plans may prove to be a damp squib if the angry kids have their way. Meanwhile, the bulldozers are quiet, waiting for work to do . . .

Ringleaders Val Bryant and Joe Crabtree insist that they are just good friends united in a worthy cause. The business company says, 'The problem is just a minor setback.' This paper will see . . .

'What do you think about that, then?' said a triumphant Val, pushing the newspaper under Bob's nose. 'If that isn't fame, I don't know what is.'

'Criminal fame,' said Bob, barely glancing, his mouth full of scrambled eggs. 'I heard the police arrested you, then let you go. Real fame is when the police are protecting you from screaming fans.'

'It would be a famously good idea if you two stopped lounging over that kitchen table and washed the breakfast dishes in my famous sink,' said their mum. She spoke to her flushed and proud daughter. 'Tip-toe up the stairs and bring down your father's breakfast tray. He's probably fallen back to sleep over *The Financial Times*. Try not to wake the poor, tired man.'

'They've done well, though,' said Bob, admiringly. 'Because those kids took my advice, of course. They've certainly got the money-men on the run. Right, Mum, out of the way. I'll show you how to wash-up. But I'll need some of that stuff that's kind to your hands. I need to protect my guitar-picking nails, you see.'

'I'm going round to Angela's house,' said Val, returning with her father's empty tray. 'And he's fallen back to sleep over the crossword puzzle with two answers filled in and both wrong . . .'

The Hopkins owned the poshest house in the road. It was mock-timbered and with little round bottled panes at every window. Val rang the bell and was ushered inside by Angela. Cyril grinned and gave his thumbs-up sign, though he still looked shaky after his swinging experience on the metal ball.

'Any news?' asked Val. 'Apart from our fame in the newspaper? Has your dad found a loophole in the law yet?'

'Well,' said Angela, cautiously. 'He came home very late last night. When Mum asked him where he'd been he said, 'Can't talk now dear, I'm busy,' then he went into his study and shut the door.'

'Then this morning he came down and gulped

a cup of tea, all at a dash,' said Cyril, puzzled. 'When Mum asked where he was going at such a pace he said, "Don't bother me dear, I've work to do." Then he hared out of the house and roared away in his roller without saying goodbye.'

'That sounds promising,' said Val. 'He's probably found a loophole in the law and is busy driving his coach-and-horses through it. I just hope he doesn't demand a huge fee from us children, win or lose.'

'Our dad wouldn't do that,' promised Angela. 'Anyway, our pocket-money wouldn't even get his car washed.'

'So, what shall we do today?' said Cyril. 'While we're waiting to hear some good news? Sunday can be such a boring day.'

'We could take a stroll through The Dingles and over the old stone bridge,' said Val. 'In this time of crisis we're allowed to cross over. We could even call in on our new allies, the Crabtrees.'

'Good idea,' said Cyril. 'I've heard the Crabtrees keep chickens. Not frozen ones but those with feathers on. I'd like to see them.'

Five minutes later they were on their way. Cyril

had his personal copy of *The Lord Of The Rings* under his arm, plus his powerful torch in his pocket. They stopped at the newsagents where Val bought some Mars-bars. Then they were soon wading through the tall tiger-grass, their eyes nervously alert for anything striped lying in wait . . .

'Don't think I'm having a picnic up here,' shouted Billy, lowering down a long cord. 'I've been surviving on salted peanuts all night. The thieving squirrels pinched most of them.'

'We understand the hardship you're suffering, Billy,' soothed Val. 'Here are the supplies you asked for. And if the wind starts blowing your tree about we'll bring you some seasick pills,' and packing all the items into a plastic shopping-bag she tied them to the cord. With a cheerful grin Billy whisked them up into his leafy nest.

'What number is the Crabtree house?' mused Val. Then they saw Buff lying outside a front gate, his head in his paws. He growled softly as they approached, but he didn't attack as they patted him and walked down the path and knocked the knocker. A lady who looked astonishingly like Joe opened the door and smiled uncertainly. Introducing themselves, the three were ushered in.

A comfortable chaos met their eyes. A jumble of books and toys littered the carpet. The telly was blaring out a violent Tom and Jerry cartoon. Seeing their unexpected visitors, the sprawled Crabtree kids fell quiet and looked rather embarrassed. Joe jumped to his feet and switched off the telly. Not knowing what to expect, Mrs Crabtree hurried into the kitchen to make tea. The awkward silence was broken by Christie.

'Hop it!' he shouted, pointing a dripping egg-soldier at the three. Buff who had slunk in with the visitors, looked up at his master and barked loyally. Christie looked so serious that it was funny. Everyone dissolved into laughter including a relieved Mrs Crabtree who was listening from the kitchen. The children made room for the trio on the battered settee and armchairs. Sipping her tea, Val explained why they had come. Firstly to say that they'd delivered Billy's supplies, and second to ask if they had seen the newspaper, and what did they think of their sudden fame? Jakey, who had his nose deep in *The Pickwick Papers* glanced up.

'I hope no one gets sued for being innocent,' he sighed. 'Poor Mr Pickwick . . .'

'Though I think they should have used more pictures than just the one of Billy up his tree,' complained Josie. 'After all, what did he do but grin down through leaves while the rest of us were defending the bridge?'

'It was rather a waste of film,' agreed Angela. 'I was snapped dozens of times from my left side, but I'm not in the newspaper.'

'The important thing is our cause has made news,' said Joe. 'It doesn't matter whose picture is in the paper. It's all helping to save The Dingles from the Company.'

'I agree,' said Val, quickly. 'I begged the photographer not to snap me but he was like a vulture. Heaven knows how the Hollywood stars cope with it. By the way, what shall we do by way of plans this morning, Joe? Perhaps we should check the cherry-tree in The Secret Wood to see it's all right.'

'Why shouldn't it be all right?' said Joe, suspiciously. 'I'm not having the yellow-hammers disturbed. Anyway, Billy will holler from his tree if the enemy launch a sneak attack.'

'There's never much to do on Sundays,' sighed Josie. 'Apart from biting your nails and twiddling your thumbs.'

'Our dad is working very hard this morning,' ventured Cyril. He dodged Christie's attempt to push an egg-soldier up his nose. 'And all for our cause. We've never seen him so high-powered before. At this moment he's probably down at the Council Records Office trying to build our case from nothing. He's determined to overthrow the plans for the supermarket. And the amazing thing is, he's doing it all for nothing. He isn't like our dad any more.'

'He looked saint-like when he left home this morning,' said Angela. 'As if he was going out to fight some evil monster. And he's doing it all for nothing!' Jakey looked over the top of his Dickens book and raised an eyebrow. He knew that legal people didn't work for nothing, especially on Sundays. He could see everyone's pocket-money for the next five years gurgling down the drain as Mr Hopkins fleeced them all.

'So, there's nothing we can do until the deadline tomorrow morning,' said Joe. 'We can only hope that Mr Hopkins finds what he's looking for in the Council files. If he doesn't, then we'll have to take up our battle stations again.'

'I know what we can do,' said Josie. 'Instead of biting our nails we can all go to Sunday School with Jenny.'

Their little sister had just come in from the backyard. She had cleared out the henhouse, scattered some grain and had been pecked by the cockerel. But she didn't mind. Poultry-breeders had to put up with such things. And she had been rewarded for her efforts.

'Seven eggs this morning,' she said, proudly. 'And most of them look like double-yolkers. Some of my hens must be working the nightshift. I'm going to Sunday School now. I'm going to thank gentle Jesus for blessing my lovely chucks. And Josie, I want you to hard-boil two eggs and throw them up to Billy in his tree. Not the large brown speckly one. That's for the constable when he comes calling on me again. See you later . . . cluck . . . cluck . . .' and she snatched up her coloured Gospel story-book and raced away. No one offered to go with her. Jenny didn't mind. She knew some people were shy about singing hymns as loudly as they could. She was quite content listening to her own voice and thinking her own thoughts . . .

'So, all we can do is wait and hope that Mr Hopkins comes up with the goods,' said Joe.

'Yet you feel so helpless doing nothing,' sighed Val.

'I've got plenty you lot can do,' said Mrs Crabtree, poking her head around the kitchen door. 'If you'll peel me some potatoes and shell me some peas I've got a nice piece of steak for lunch. And I'll make one of my special Yorkshire puddings.'

'Thank you, Mrs Crabtree,' chorused the three who lived on the other side of the bridge.

It was a lovely lunch. It was even lovelier with apple-crumble for afters . . .

Thirteen

CRUNCH MONDAY

While the children slept, a man in a pin-striped suit had been poring all night through piles of dusty, ancient documents. It was Mr Hopkins, who had never been so happy throughout his career. Happy – because for the first time in his life he was not working for money. He was doing it for his children and for lots of other children. At eight o'clock, while the kids were eating breakfast and readying themselves for school, his patience was rewarded. Suddenly he was doing a little jig and shouting 'eureka', startling his exhausted friend, The Clerk Of The Council. Mr Hopkins was waving a yellowing parchment he had unearthed from the records.

'This is what we've spent the night searching for,' he shouted. 'This is the coach-and-horses document I need to fight for the rights of the kids out there!'

'Well, that's a relief,' said the Clerk, mopping his brow. 'I think we deserve a nice cup of tea, don't you think?'

In school that Monday morning the kids were also startled and delighted when the Headmaster spoke to them in assembly. Not about the usual things, but about preserving the countryside. He seemed quite angry as he spoke. Not surprising, he being a keen rambler and bird-watcher . . .

'I know most of you are feeling angry about what has been happening in The Dingles these past few days,' he began. 'And so am I. Today is the day the Company men return to continue their work of destruction. I cannot advise you what to do in this situation, and nor will I. My task and the task of your teachers is to teach. But many of us support you in your protest. As I say, I cannot advise you what to do, but I have the authority to decide which subjects you should study. So, with the agreement of all the teachers I'm declaring this Monday a Countryside Research Day which means that you'll be allowed to roam wherever you wish. I'll expect you to draw diagrams and maps of course, for your teachers will be testing your experiences in the field later in the week . . .'

'Are we allowed to press flowers in our note-books?' asked Jenny, sweetly. 'And count the number of eggs in duck-nests?'

'A very good idea, Jennifer Crabtree,' smiled the Headmaster. 'And now everyone dismiss and good luck with your field studies . . .'

Amid cheers and much stamping, the school hall emptied in seconds. One boy wasn't there to hear the Headmaster's words. He had been play-ing truant all morning without his permission. The boy had also been playing truant from home, much to his mum's distress. All through the night Billy had been curled up in his tree-fortress, rea-ding *The Lord Of The Rings* by torchlight, and shar-ing his Mars-bars with the neighbouring squirrels. It was the coughing roar of an engine that brought him back into the real world. He and the squirrels peered down to see that the bulldozer driver was back in his cab and revving his cold engine. A throaty whine joined in, as the power-saw men tested their tree-felling tools.

'Had a good night, Billy?' called the bulldozer

man. 'Don't take this personally, but in two hours' time our orders are to storm your fortress and saw your tree down. An expert climber is on the way with lots of ropes to force you safely to the ground.'

'It'll take all the evil horsemen in Middle Earth to get me out of this tree,' yelled Billy. 'Leave me alone, I'm reading about magic and stuff . . .'

At the bridge the atmosphere was noisy and tense. In his cab the bulldozer driver was enjoying a bacon-and-egg sandwich as he idled his engine. He felt sympathy for the kids, but they didn't pay him . . .

Bored with waiting, the rebels against the Company put down their banners to have a paddle in the stream, saving their energy and throats for when the crunch-time arrived. It came soon enough . . .

'Right, I want all of you kids off this private land,' shouted the site-boss, jumping from his Land-Rover. 'My Company has had enough of your nuisance. I want this bridge cleared in five minutes. Mick, get ready to knock it down.

Regretfully, Mick the bulldozer man swung his heavy metal ball towards the bridge. Being just a practice swing, it merely grazed and chipped the sturdy stones. The children groaned. It seemed all the placards and protest in the world could not prevent what was about to happen. But unbeknown to them, help was on the way, though they were to face more misery first. Up the track came the Company man in his Company car. Behind him lurched a van-load of security men. Piling out of their vehicle, the security men formed a menacing line behind the Company man as he addressed the kids.

'I have kiddies of my own,' he smarmed. 'So I can quite understand your high spirits Now, you've had your fun. Go back to school and let my men get on with their work.'

'If this bridge dies, so will we,' shouted Joe, defiantly.

'Right,' said the angered site-boss. He snapped at Mick and pointed. 'Smash that bridge down!'

Mick was just preparing to make a serious swing at the old stones when . . .

After Mr Hopkins had shouted 'eureka' and done his little jig, he and the Clerk scrambled into the Roller to pick up their friend the Inspector. Speeding down the track that led to the bridge, they arrived in a squeal of brakes and much spitting of mud. They were just in time. The security men had pushed the kids from the bridge and Mick was swinging his metal ball for real this time . . .

'Stop,' shouted the Inspector. 'All work on this site must cease. The Clerk Of The Council has something important to say.'

The Clerk glanced apologetically at the glaring Company man. Then he spoke to everyone. 'It seems a dreadful mistake has been made. At the insistence of Mr Hopkins the solicitor, I went through the council archives once again. Together we discovered an old document. But let Mr Hopkins tell you himself . . .'

The children gazed hopefully at Mr Hopkins as he stepped forward and cleared his throat. His usually neat suit was crumpled, his sleek hair was rumpled after his sleepless night rummaging through the archives. But his cheeks glowed pink with the fire of passion. With a dramatic gesture he produced a rolled-up document from his pocket.

'Our dad's going to say something important,' said proud Angela to Josie. 'He's got a lovely way with words when he's talking about something he believes in.'

'Good old Dad,' whispered Cyril. 'I knew you wouldn't let us down.'

'To quote . . .' boomed Mr Hopkins, putting on his spectacles and unrolling the yellowing document . . .

'Dated this day the fourteenth of August 1829. This being a late addition to my Will and Testament. That I Sir Charles Crabtree hereby bequeath the land on my Chinnbrook estate known as The Dingles and containing The Secret Wood and the old stone bridge to the children of the area that they may enjoy its delights for generations to come. I deliver this land into their safekeeping in the hope that they will guard with their love the precious trees and wildlife living there.

I dedicated The Secret Wood to the memory of my dear daughter Gertie who dreamed her dreams in that magic place and tragically died just one month ago. As my beloved and loving daughter she will always be the Queen Gertie of her fantasy which she acted out with her friends in joyous times.

I entreat the children who come after to tend her magic cherry-tree and when the fruit ripens, eat and think of her. For she is ever in her Secret Wood in spirit if not in earthly form.

Sir Charles Crabtree
the fourteenth of August 1829

'End of quote,' finished Mr Hopkins, looking very moved. 'This document is quite genuine and legal, I'll stake my reputation on it. And so will my friend the Clerk Of The Council stake his job on it.'

'Perfectly true,' said the flustered Clerk.

The angry Company man barged in to examine the document for himself. Clever as he was, he could pick no holes in it. The Will And Testament Of Sir Charles Crabtree was genuine all right. It would have taken a brain more brilliant than Mr Hopkins to drive a coach-and-horses

through it. Thankfully, the Company lacked Mr Hopkins on their side.

Then the Inspector stepped in. Waving his little cane and frowning at everyone, he said, 'I am ordering you all to disperse. Otherwise arrests will be made. I won't warn you twice!'

Like Mr Hopkins, the Inspector was enjoying his moment of glory. All through his career he had yearned to control an ugly crowd. He had dreamed of leading a baton-charge against a mob. He felt a bit disappointed. The Company man and his site-boss just looked sulky, while the faces of the children had turned from prayerful hope to beams of joy. There was nothing ugly in their manner as they punched the air to celebrate their victory.

'You haven't heard the last of this,' shouted the Company man, jumping into his swish car and throttling the engine. 'We'll take this case to the House Of Lords if we have to . . .' and he roared off.

It was bluff of course. Even the children knew that lords were in love with hunting and shooting and fishing, and had no time for anything else, except golf, which reminded Mr Hopkins and his friends the Clerk and the Inspector . . .

'Now children,' said Mr Hopkins, sternly. 'You've won your battle, now let's have you back in school tomorrow. And Angela and Cyril, I order you to get off home and scrub your filthy faces and knees.'

'Yes, Dad,' they replied, gazing adoringly at their hero. 'And we'll scrub your car when you get home tonight.'

'Thanks, Mr Hopkins,' said Joe. 'For saving the bridge and The Secret Wood.'

'You'll be Joe Crabtree,' said the man, looking keenly at the boy. 'Who Mrs Bryant talks about. My wife, Mrs Hopkins would like to meet you sometime. She dabbles in poetry herself. Perhaps you could come over one of these days? But there is something else you can do for me. When you see your brother Billy, tell him I'd be grateful to know what happened to my coin collection. I'm not accusing him mind, because there's no evidence. The coins are in a black polished case lined with blue velvet. I'd be very glad if they were returned to me.'

'I'll talk to Billy, Mr Hopkins,' promised Joe. 'But he's not a sneak-thief. He'd never climb through people's windows like a burglar. He only borrows things like the odd skate or a bike or toys that catch his fancy. Anyway, as he told the constable the other morning, he has his own coin collection.'

'Has he, indeed?' said Mr Hopkins, raising an eyebrow. 'And where is Billy at this moment?'

'He's up a tree still defending The Dingles against the bulldozers,' said Josie, proudly. 'He's played his part in this fight, like everyone else.'

'Don't tell me which tree,' smiled Mr Hopkins. 'In case I'm tempted to coax him down myself. But appeal to him, please. You see, I've collected my coins since I was a boy myself, and I'm lost without them.' Then with a wave to the smiling kids, he and the Clerk and the Inspector climbed into his Rolls Royce and sped away to play another round of golf.

'Three cheers for Mr Hopkins whose brilliant mind has saved The Dingles for generations to come,' cried Val. 'Hip, hip . . .'

'Fancy cheering the back of a vanishing car,'

said Josie, shaking her head. 'You always go over the top, Val Bryant.'

'You've got nothing to be cheerful about, Val,' said Angela, sadly. 'According to the Will of Sir Charles, Queen Gertie was his dear daughter who invented the story for her and her friends to act out. So the ghost of the lady we saw drifting through The Secret Wood was not a medieval queen. Which leaves your theory in tatters, I'm afraid.'

'Which means that the glitter we spied inside the hollow cherry-tree was probably just a toffee-paper blown in by the wind,' said Cyril, disappointed.

'Faint hearts,' scorned Val. 'I don't give up. I still believe in the ancient legend. And I'll never give up my historical quest until I've proved it. And Joe will help me, won't you Joe?'

'Don't you mean, Sir Joe?' said Josie, mischievously. 'Sir Charles Crabtree owned all the land around here and then his line seemed to die out. But did it? Don't you think it strange that we modern Crabtrees have always lived around Chinnbrook Wood? Perhaps our Joe, the eldest son in our family is a long-lost heir, or something?'

'Joe Crabtree, with noble blood?' said Val, rising haughtily to the bait. 'And living in an ordinary house? I don't think so!'

'But just look at Joe's profile,' said Josie, trying not to giggle. 'Don't you think he looks snooty and romantic leaning over the bridge deep in thought, his hair blowing in the breeze?'

'Nonsense,' snapped Val. 'The Crabtree name is just a coincidence. As for his profile, it looks very ordinary to me.'

But Val was lying. To her eyes Joe's profile was something to behold. He looked a bit like Heathcliff from *Wuthering Heights* except in colour instead of black and white. In fact, Joe was wrapped in his thoughts, relishing a victory won, and taking a few quiet moments to compose the start of a poem. It would be about the kids and the yellow-hammers and the plants and the small animals who would own The Secret Wood for ever. Then he snapped from his dream to become no-nonsense Joe again.

'Billy,' he said, abruptly. 'He's still high in that

tree. We must get him down, I need to talk to him. And Mum will be worrying. Josie, run on ahead. Coax him down and tell him the battle is over.'

'Joe,' said Val, widening her yellow-hammer eyes. 'After our victory, can I now visit The Secret Wood whenever I want?'

'You've earned it,' said Joe, generously. 'And Angela and Cyril. But I must be there when you do. You won't know where to tread, you see. I can't stand clumsy feet in The Secret Wood. But we can discuss it later. Now I'm off, for me and my family have a problem.'

'Ah, the Billy problem,' sighed Angela. 'About my dad's rare coins. But everyone knows Billy. He'll borrow skates and bikes and things, but I don't think he'd creep into houses to steal, for Billy has a harmless style of pinching we quite like.'

'Billy can have my next new bike for keeps,' said Cyril, kindly. 'Dad will always buy me next year's model. For Billy risked his life in the tree to stop the bulldozer and the chainsaw men cutting The Secret Wood down. He deserves our thanks.'

'If Billy wasn't still up his tree I'd give him a kiss,' said Angela, warmly.

'Billy wouldn't like that,' Joe smiled. He turned and hurried after Josie. 'But I must go and talk to him before the constable calls at our house again.'

'How about a picnic in The Secret Wood Saturday afternoon?' shouted Val after him. 'We could bring sandwiches and coke, and you could stare at the yellow-hammers through Cyril's powerful binoculars. In the meantime I could do some vital tapping and measuring of the ancient cherry-tree . . .'

But Joe was dashing away, and didn't hear.

'Let's get home,' said Angela to Cyril. 'We promised Dad we've have a good wash and scrub.'

'You're right,' agreed Cyril. 'We've done a good job here today. We can all be happy that we played our part in saving these precious places.'

'For us and the children who come after,' nodded Val.

Tired and grubby but proud, the three crossed back over the bridge to the narrow path that wound towards the tiger-grass, that led to home . . .

Starting up his monster machine, Mick chugged it towards the road and his next job. He was joined in convoy by his mate in his snapping-jaws bulldozer and the chainsaw men in their jeep, leaving an undefeated Billy high in his tree with chapters of *The Lord Of The Rings* to read, and Mars-bars to spare. Josie arrived . . .

'We've won the day, Billy,' she appealed into the branches. 'Come down, Mum is worried about you. She's cooking your favourite tea for a treat.'

'I'm stopping here until I've finished my book,' yelled Billy. 'Anyway, bulldozers aren't to be trusted. They sometimes sneak back in the dead of night. I don't care if the cruel riders in my book get me. It's these nibbling squirrels I'm worried about – they've already chewed the rubber off my trainers. Tell Mum to give my tea to Buff. Tell him I said he can have it or he might get hiccups from guilt.'

The girl knew it was hopeless trying to persuade Billy to do something he didn't want to do. She shrugged her shoulders as Joe joined her.

'Billy,' he warned. 'You're still under suspicion over the rare coin affair. I need to talk to you about it. Come down and let's go home and thrash it out. The constable is bound to call again.'

'I didn't pinch Mr Hopkins' stupid old coins,' said Billy, angrily. 'I've got my own collection that's going to pay for Mum's cruise around the world. Just go away and leave me alone . . .' and he pulled up his rope-ladder to show his determination to stay.

Joe and Josie were wasting their time. Slowly they wended their way home, their thoughts troubled for Billy. Oh, please that he wasn't lying about the missing coins . . . The welcoming glow from the windows of their house cheered them up a bit. Their worried mother would also be in need of cheering up when she heard that Billy was still a suspected burglar. As they explained the good news and the bad, Buff was having a violent attack of hiccups after gobbling down yet another huge meal from the absent Billy's plate. Though much enjoyed, Buff's guilt was plain as he burped quietly from his box.

Fourteen

A Fair And Handsome Cop

At dusk Jenny slipped out of the house carrying a plastic bag. Inside was a soapy flannel to wash a dirty face, the morning's copy of the *Beano*, plus a freshly-baked egg pie. Arriving at the foot of the tree she raised her head and made a soft clucking sound. It was the chicken signal that she and Billy often used when secrecy was important.

'Oh, it's you,' said Billy, peering down. 'What's in the bag?'

'Supplies to help you last out,' whispered Jenny. 'Lower your string and I'll tie them on. There are two cans of coke as well.'

'How's Mum?' asked the boy. He sounded concerned. 'She doesn't believe I stole the coins, does she, Jen?'

'None of us do,' said his sister, fiercely. 'But we're all agreed that you must face the music and the handsome constable sooner or later. I think you should face him sooner, for he's very kind.'

'I'll think about it,' said Billy, hauling up the bag.' Just tell Mum that I'm innocent and not to worry. I'll come down when the time is right.'

'Message received . . . cluck . . . cluck . . .' hissed Jenny. She looked up expectantly. 'Well, you haven't forgotten the code for "over and out" . . . ?'

'Cluck . . . cluck . . .' called Billy, obediently.

'That wasn't too hard, was it?' said the girl, turning and racing back along the track for home.

Billy had been wishing for some time that *The Lord Of The Rings* had been a lot thinner. There were so many characters and twists and turns to fit inside one brain. Jakey would have read it in a day plus a night with a torch under the bed-clothes, but Billy would never have his small brother's genius. So it was with pleasure he began to read his favourite *Beano* comic. As he read he took a large bite out of Jenny's egg-pie. He grimaced and clutched his jaw. The pastry was as hard as iron. His sister had meant well, but she couldn't cook like Mum. For an experiment he crumbled the pie

157

on to the rickety planks of his tree-fortress. Just as he expected, the squirrels loved Jenny's baking, but then they were used to cracking hard nuts. He was just finishing off a can of coke when he heard a clumsy rustling sound from the bushes below.

'The Dark Riders!' whispered Billy, terrified. 'They've come for me!'

Frightened out of his wits, he peered down. He could see a dark shape moving through the undergrowth. It wasn't a badger, for they moved quietly. For the first time since beginning his defiant stand, the boy felt sheer terror. What could it be? Then as his eyes became accustomed to the dark he could see that the shape was human and horseless. The shadowy figure slipped into The Secret Wood. Overcoming his fear, Billy quietly paid out his rope-ladder and clambered to the ground. Then with the stealth and cunning of a Red Indian stalker, he set off to track the interloper down . . .

Arriving at the centre of the wood, Billy was puzzled to see in the moonlight a little man dressed completely in black, crouched at the foot of the cherry-tree. He watched as the man reached into his shoulder-satchel and pulled out a small, gleaming axe. With swift strokes he began to chop through the peeling bark and rotting wood towards the hollow within. Billy was filled with anger. How dare this creeping stranger hack into the cherry-tree where a private secret lay hidden!

The boy came to a decision. He needed help. As quickly as he could, he retraced his steps and hared for home. He knew that whatever happened the world would soon learn about the secret he had kept close to his chest for so long. Yet the outrage of a trespasser hacking at the cherry-tree over-rode his personal secret. Joe should know, and Joe would know what to do, he said over and over to himself as his feet pounded over road and pavement.

Seconds later he was hammering on the front door of his house, his chest heaving, gasping for breath. As Joe opened the door his little brother fell inside, words tumbling out.

'A strange man in The Secret Wood . . . chopping at the old cherry-tree . . . he must have found out about something hidden there . . .'

he wheezed. 'But that doesn't matter now, it's the tree we've got to save!'

After some alarmed questioning from Joe and Josie, it became clear from Billy's story that something awful was taking place in the wood. Quickly Josie dialled the police-station and was answered by Jenny's handsome boyfriend. He listened intently then snapped orders back. The Crabtree children should stay at home while the police dealt with this matter. Then he rang off. It wasn't on, of course . . .

Having been woken by all the noise, Jenny crept sleepily downstairs. When she learnt that Josie had been chatting with her very own personal constable, she became wide-awake. It was a mass disobedience of police orders as the Crabtrees pulled on their boots and anoraks. After promising their worried mother that everything was all right, and after much slamming of the front door and garden gate, a file of Crabtrees vanished into the night – towards The Secret Wood.

Jenny's constable, who had sped there in his patrol-car, was a bit annoyed when the children crept into the thick bush near the cherry-tree beside him. Though at this point in his detective work he could only hiss for them to stay quiet as he observed the little dark man. The suspect was still chopping away at the trunk of the cherry-tree, unaware that he was being watched. Suddenly he gave a satisfied grunt. Putting away his hatchet he reached into the hacked-away hollow and began to pull things out, quickly stuffing them into his bag. At this point, with Jenny clinging to his hand, the young constable pushed from the bush and advanced to make an arrest . . .

'It's a fair cop,' said the little, wispy man after jumping with fear and surprise. He offered his wrists to be handcuffed. 'I've had a good run, and now I can have a good rest in the nick. I wish you to take into account at least twenty other breaking-in jobs I've done in the area.'

More policemen arrived, including the Inspector who had been interrupted in the middle of a Golf Club Ball. With him was Mr Hopkins, who had also been enjoying that evening out.

The contents of the little man's satchel were

amazing. Out spilled a wealth of necklaces, dia-mond rings, gold wristwatches and two priceless French clocks, plus a velvet-lined case containing rows of glittering coins. Indeed, as admitted, the burglar known as 'Slinky Slim' had been robbing all over the district for a long time. He confessed he had been dropping his booty into the hollow of the cherry-tree to be picked up later. Unfortu-nately he had chosen the wrong night, thanks to watchful Billy and the constable who had been so quick off the mark.

Mr Hopkins was overjoyed. He approached the small grimy boy who many believed had stolen the coin collection. Ruffling Billy's hair, the man said he was deeply sorry for thinking ill of him, and that tomorrow he was taking Billy into town to buy him the latest mountain-bike, even later than Cyril's. A bike of the future, no less . . .

'How many gears?' asked Billy, delighted.

'As many as you want,' said Mr Hopkins, clutching his precious coin-case to his chest.

Jenny was over the moon when the Inspector congratulated her blushing young constable for his detective work and swift arrest. He even hinted that if the young man cared to join the Golf Club, his path to promotion would be smoothed. 'Slinky Slim' seemed quite happy to be led away in handcuffs. He had lots of friends in prison he was looking forward to seeing again . . .

'I always knew Billy was innocent,' wept Mrs Crabtree when her children, plus Billy, came home to break the good news.

'The ass of a law has got it right for once,' shouted Jakey from the top of the stairs. 'Our Billy could easily have been transported to Australia for something he didn't do. Instead he's getting a brand-new bike, which is justice in my eyes. I just hope the law dosen't slip up again and arrest the bike for belonging to Billy.'

'Hop it!' yelled Christie, his head and dummy poking through the stair-railings. 'Me and Buff are trying to sleep. Unless we get two bowls of cocoa and some chocolate biscuits we're going to bark all night.'

Mrs Crabtree happily prepared the late-night snack. She was also happy that little Christie had found his tongue for other words at last. She made herself a cup of cocoa and, loading the tray, went to bed.

'Billy,' said Joe, curiously. 'I was watching you while the police were examining the stolen loot. Why were you standing with your back pressed against the hole chopped in the cherry-tree? I saw something else.'

'So did I,' said Josie, looking keenly at Jenny. 'I saw you sneak under cover of Billy's back and reach inside the tree. What was in that Oxo-tin you stuffed into your anorak?'

'Mind your own business,' smiled Billy, mysteriously. 'It's hidden away in another safe place that only me and Jenny know about.'

'Cluck . . . cluck,' giggled Jenny, enjoying her share of the secret.

'Well, if that's all you've got to say, get off to bed,' said Joe, sternly. 'And don't be late up, it's school in the morning.'

It had been a long and eventful night. Joe and Josie sat sipping cocoa and discussing the surprises that were just beginning to sink in. Billy was now a hero instead of the burglar some

164

people had thought him to be. They agreed he fully deserved the brand-new bike Mr Hopkins was taking him to buy. One thing was certain, Billy would never need to borrow one again. But knowing their little brother, well . . . for the borrowing was deep in him.

'Joe,' said Josie, slowly. Her eyes sparkled mischievously. 'Later on when the police and everyone had gone, I was watching you. Deny that you also had a rummage around in the hollow tree. So what were you searching for?'

'Whatever it was, it's found,' grinned Joe. 'And will remain there until tomorrow night after tea.'

'I'd ask what that means, but I won't bother,' laughed Josie. Then she was serious. 'But I'd still like to know what was in the Oxo-tin Billy and Jenny took from the tree. And where is it now? But I'm off to bed. Good night, Joe.'

'Good night,' said the boy.

Alone for the first time that day, Joe settled beside the small night lamp to write another verse of the poem he intended to call 'Tiger-Grass and Tigers'.

The oak we climbed and straddled,
How carried sound then,
Enemies all took by crocodiles . . .
Then mothers hailed but who had time for tea
When we had King Kong weeping up a tree,
Begging for compromise?'

Joe closed his notebook and yawned. Then he rose and went to the window and gazed out into the night. He was observed. The owl on the branch hooted a welcome to the night he ruled, huge eyes intent upon his friend.

'Beware, there are tigers in the tiger-grass out there, old owl,' whispered Joe.

'Take care that you don't meet your match, for I'd miss you very much. For what is a branch without an owl, or an owl without a branch? Now I'll hoot you goodnight for I'm very tired . . .'

And the bird hooted back, before silently gliding away . . .

Fifteen

A Stroll Through The Secret Wood

The next morning in assembly was special. Everyone was excitedly discussing the news about the goings-on in The Secret Wood the previous night. All kinds of rumours were being passed around as the children waited for the Headmaster to stride in and deliver his pep-talk for the day. The Art Teacher was seated at his little organ ready to launch into 'Morning Has Broken', his favourite hymn, a singalong favourite of the children too. Joe and Josie were amongst the packed crowd being patted on the back, much to their embarrassment. Val was gazing at Joe like an adoring gazelle, while Cyril pushed across to punch his arm as one mate to another.

Then Joe and Josie were forgotten as the school's most popular hero swaggered in, late as usual.

It was Billy, complete with a sailor's roll. The sensible children realised that Billy had earned his sea-legs perched up a tree, the swaying motion being similar to a ship at sea. To the annoyance of the Art Teacher, Billy mounted the stage and began to give a lecture about the loneliness of tree-living. Survival he said, was having *The Lord Of The Rings* and the *Beano*, plus a strong torch to read them by. He also advised the wisdom of Mars-bars against egg pies. Most important was to have a strong rope-ladder to swarm down in order to stalk desperate burglars, to hand over to the police.

Then the small hero stripped his sleeve and showed his scars, and said, 'These wounds I suffered during the battle against the King of the Squirrels and his hordes. They attacked and attacked again, but I never gave up, clawed to ribbons though I was—'

'They look like flea-bites to me, Billy,' a girl giggled from the crowd. 'But I'll ignore your lies because living up a tree is bound to dizzy your thoughts.'

To the Art Teacher's relief, the Headmaster

entered the hall and stepped up to the podium. With a smile he patted Billy on the head and ordered him to scoot back and join his classmates in the crush. Then the much-respected man spoke.

'Children, much has gone on these past few days. The disruption of our school, the missing of lessons, in short, anarchy . . .' he smiled again. 'But from that anarchy has come the saving of a precious part of our countryside. Joe Crabtree tried to teach us that just one gorse bush sheltering just one nest of yellow-hammers is equally important to the learning about right-angled triangles and sliced-up circles. Now that The Dingles and The Secret Wood belongs to you all, I ask you to respect the wildlife and plants living there. For that beautiful place is your heritage, and the heritage of children to come, thanks to the generosity of the late Sir Charles Crabtree. And now let us all join hands and think of that as we sing our favourite hymn.'

The eager Art Teacher blasted out the opening notes on his organ. 'Morning Has Broken' echoed through the hall, rattling the tiles on the school roof. The words were sung lustily and happily, for this was a united school sincerely singing . . .

At lunchtime an astonishing thing happened. With all eyes upon him Joe rose from his usual table and carried his plate of pie and chips to Val's table, where he plonked it down beside her salad. Then he sat next to her and began to talk quietly. Sitting opposite, Angela and Cyril craned to hear the words that were being exchanged, but there was little clue. For the rest of the schoolday rumour went this way and that. When pressed, Joe and Val simply smiled and said nothing. Only Josie seemed to have guessed what was going on, but she kept her own counsel. It was all very vexing for Angela and Cyril and the other kids who had long known about the war between Joe and Val. What was going on? Then it was time to go home, the gossip continuing. After tea it was homework time and the curiosity faded – a little . . .

It was a nice Indian-summer evening. Bob was lounging over the kitchen table devouring a banana-sandwich that dwarfed his hand, though not his mouth. His sister was nibbling sliced tomato and lettuce on brown bread. Mrs Bryant checked her oven and was pleased to see that her egg-and-bacon pie promised to be as light as a feather. She turned from her hot toils . . .

'Oh, you're wearing that lovely frock,' she said, surprised. 'And what's all this dressing up for?'

'Val's probably gone man-mad,' grinned Bob. 'Or is it Joe-mad? We in the top class have heard all the talk.'

'Nice Joe Crabtree?' said Mrs Bryant, pleased. 'Is it he you're looking nice for? But then you must have lots to talk about after working so closely to save The Dingles. Are you going out to meet him, then?'

'I haven't said anything,' said Val, crossly. 'Can't I put on my new frock without all this fuss?'

'Well,' said Bob, teasing. 'At this time of the day you're usually flopping around in my old tee-shirts. I'm used to seeing you look like a bag of spuds tied in the middle.'

'Don't you say I'm fat,' flared Val. 'Anyway, it's better than being a skeleton like you.'

'Now then,' warned their mum. 'I've told you before about wars in my kitchen. I'm trying to watch my pastry to see it doesn't burn.'

'I'm going now, anyway,' said Val, pushing back her chair. 'See you, Mum. As for you, Bob Bryant, I hope I never see you again!' and out she flounced looking pretty in her frock to keep her secret date.

'What did I say?' said Bob, indignantly. 'Can't she take a joke? I was only trying to help.'

'If you want to help, get cracking on that sinkful of pots and pans,' said his mum, handing him her rubber-gloves.

Pulling them on, Bob good-naturedly tackled the washing-up. While he scrubbed and rinsed, he dreamed about the moment when his band would hit the big-time. Then there would be no more drudgery for his Mum – nor his Dad for that matter.

'Best shirt, smart trousers,' said Mrs Crabtree handing them freshly ironed to her eldest son.

'Is there anything else our Sir Joseph Crabtree desires? Dare I ask where he's going?'

'He's not doing his Pip from *Great Expectations* again!' said a disgusted Jakey, looking over the top of his book. 'I'd say more, but I'm deep into *Hard Times*.'

Joe looked so wonderfully smart that Christie grinned and shouted 'bighead' while Buff worried the leg of Joe's new trousers. Just then Josie burst into the room carrying an old Oxo-tin, looking extremely excited. An angry Billy and a tearful Jenny followed close behind.

'I was determined to find out what these two were up to,' said Josie, triumphantly. She brandished the Oxo-tin. 'This is what they sneaked away from the hollow in the cherry-tree. And I also found this . . .'

'What could that be?' said Mrs Crabtree, peering at the machine in her daughter's hand. 'An old-fashioned vacuum-cleaner? Where were they hidden, Josie?'

'Only in Jenny's hen-house,' said her daughter, annoyed. 'And we were so proud of our Billy last night and this morning. Now we find he's got a box of hidden loot and a machine that he probably uses to crack safes. But most awful of all, he's roped Jenny in as his accomplice. Jenny whose whole life revolves around poultry-breeding and Sunday School!'

'Oh, Billy . . . Billy . . .' said Mrs Crabtree, shaking her head in sorrow. 'How could you?'

'Wait a bit,' said Joe. He was examining the strange machine. Then he began to laugh. He turned to his little brother. 'Tell them what it is.'

'It's a metal-detector I bought from the Army and Navy Stores in the village,' said the boy, his eyes bright. 'And I used every penny from saving my pocket-money to buy it, Mum.'

'But what were you using it for?' asked his mother, mystified.

'To detect enough money under the ground to take you on a world trip around the world,' said Billy, proudly. 'And I think I've got enough. I've been tracking down treasure on the waste-ground by the rubbish-dump every night after school.'

'And is this the treasure you've detected with your machine?' said Josie, rather cruelly as she opened the Oxo-tin and spilled the contents over the carpet. Out spilled a torrent of coins, of strange shapes and sizes. It was the sum collection of Billy's life he had moved so carefully from hiding place to hiding place. And every coin was meant to enable his mum to relax on a posh liner for the holiday of her life. Mrs Crabtree's eyes moistened as she stared at the hoarded coins. She recognised so many. There were lots of old copper pennies, scatterings of ancient half-crowns, plus shilling pieces and sixpences. Also tiny farthings with a jenny wren on one side and a stern-looking king on the other.

'We used to call this money pounds, shilling and pence,' said Mrs Crabtree gently to Billy. 'My mum and dad would shop with it when I was your age. In those days a penny would buy a sherbet or a stick of licorice.'

'What's this clump of coins all stuck together?' said Joe, holding a lump of metal up to the light. 'They're all caked in hardened mud, but you can't mistake the glint of gold shining through. Have we still got Dad's magnifying-glass?'

Jakey ran to get it from the drawer.

Joe scratched at the congealed clump of coins and peered. Suddenly one of them broke away and rolled free across the floor. Mrs Crabtree held it up to the light.

'I do believe this is an ancient sovereign!' she said, excitedly. 'My granddad had one on his watchchain. How many more has Billy got?'

'Dozens,' said Joe, breaking the petrified lump into bits. The family watched, dumb-struck, as the sovereigns rolled glinting gold over the floor.

'They could be enormously valuable,' said Josie in an awed voice. 'Billy could easily be very rich. All the golden sovereigns on earth belonged to Queen Victoria. She kept them all in a private drawer.'

'I know,' said Billy, proudly. 'But I found some to build my collection. I'm thinking of selling all my coins to Mr Hopkins to get the money for Mum's cruise around the world.'

'I'll take Billy and his sovereigns round to Mr Hopkins' house,' said Josie, firmly.

'In the meantime, Joe, you go out on your date with Val Bryant and slay her with your charm!'

Before her eldest son could utter another word Mrs Crabtree ushered him to the front door. Kissing his cheek and patting his back, she urged him away . . .

They met as arranged that morning on the old stone bridge, that early evening. The breeze was soft and the birds were chirruping, boasting of their full bellies as they readied themselves for sleep. In The Secret Wood a badger began to bumble along a favoured trail, two little ones hurrying behind. In a bush a drab nightingale cleared its throat to wait for the rising of the moon, to let rip with gorgeous song. And in the tangled gorse around the cherry-tree the yellow-hammers perched, singing 'little-bit-of-bread-and-no-cheese' as yellow-hammers always did, and ever would.

Joe and Val approached the cherry-tree looming majestically in the centre of The Secret Wood, its old boughs bowed, its new sprouts hung with blood-red fruit. The freshly-hacked hole in its lovely old trunk caused Val to shudder.

'How horrible, Joe,' she said. 'Poor little Gertie

Crabtree, that her cherry-tree would be slashed open like that!'

'Perhaps it was meant to be . . . perhaps she hoped it would be, some day,' said Joe, mysteriously. 'Perhaps she hid her secret, but hoped it would be discovered one day in the future, to bring it to life again.'

'I don't understand,' said Val, puzzled.

'Put your hand inside the hollow,' challenged Joe. 'Unless you're too scared!'

'Dare away, you don't frighten me,' said Val. She plunged her hand and her arm into the darkness, her fingers groping. A look of wonder came over her face as she withdrew her mould-covered arm. She was clutching an oil-papered wrapped parcel. Amazed, she stared at it. Joe who had found it the night before, watched as she opened it. It was a red, leather-bound book entitled in gold on the cover . . .

THE DIARY AND PLAYS
OF GERTRUDE CRABTREE

The diary was crammed with the spidery writing of a girl who had lived her short life in a world of fantasy. There were jottings of plays and the roles she and her friends would act out. The diary said, rather sadly, that she was an only child, and the love for her parents was evident throughout. Mostly her love and devotion was centred around The Secret Wood and the old cherry-tree. She wrote with delight about the badgers rolling about their business, and about her yellow-hammers singing away in the gorse bushes. From entry to entry she wrote about the play she had written. It would be called 'Queen Gertie And Her Golden Rolling-Pin' in which she would play the lead, her friends the other roles. The diary went on to say that now it was autumn, and her play had been a huge success performed before her parents and the villagers of Chinnbrook Wood. Then her writing began to slope downwards as if in despair. As day followed day, each entry faltered, almost finally dying. The last entry was an appeal to someone who would come after . . .

THE DOCTOR SAYS I AM VERY ILL. I HEARD HIM WHISPERING TO MY PARENTS WHEN

THEY THOUGHT I WAS ASLEEP. THE WORDS, 'WILL NOT LAST LONG' RING IN MY MIND.

FINAL NOTE TO THIS DIARY. I AM POST-ING THIS DIARY INTO THE HOLLOW OF MY MAGICAL CHERRY-TREE IN THE HOPE THAT SOME FUTURE CHILD WILL FIND IT AND CONTINUE MY DREAMS.

I HAVE VISITED THE SECRET WOOD FOR THE LAST TIME. EVERYTHING THAT IS LEFT OF ME, MAY IT BE GUARDED BY THIS NOBLE TREE. EAT ITS FRUIT AND PRAY FOR ME.

Gertrude Crabtree 1829

'The diary of the real Queen Gertie,' said Val, awed. 'And brought to life by a girl who lived so long ago. Yet she was only acting, Joe.'

'Acting or not, she was the real thing,' said Joe, gently. Then he reached into the hollow and pulled something else out.

'Queen Gertie's Golden Rolling-pin,' gasped Val, clutching it. 'And see, Joe, there are still flecks of gold clinging to it.'

On the roughly-shaped wood were flecks of

pantomime gold, as sad as the make-up of a dying girl, of a young actress who would never see the lights and hear the cheers of fame.

'We must put it all back and seal up the hole in the cherry-tree, Joe,' urged Val. 'I don't think I'll ever write my article about Queen Gertie. I think she should be left to rest in peace.'

Joe agreed, and promised to seal everything back inside the tree. It was the proper place for them. Safe in the hollow of the cherry-tree they would remain as a memorial to the poor little rich girl who had died so young. Joe carefully smoothed out the oiled-paper and laid the treasures on it. He was about to wrap the things back up when Val stopped him. From around her neck she unfastened a silver cross on a silver chain. She placed it inside the cover of the diary and nodded for Joe to complete his task. The package was returned to the tree, Joe intending to come back the following morning to seal the hollow up again completely. Then they both ate some of the ripened cherries and spared a thought for the girl who had lived and died so long ago.

'Look,' whispered Val, excitedly pointing. 'It's

the gliding wraith again. I saw her the last time I came to The Secret Wood. It has to be the ghost of Gertrude Crabtree! See, she's dressed in a floating gown and is wearing a crown. Can't you see her, Joe? Look, she's stopped and is smiling at us.'

Joe strained his eyes to see. But the evening mist was beginning to swirl through the wood. He could only see dancing shadows as the breeze stirred the trees.

'Now she's gone,' said Val, disappointed. 'But she did smile at us. She knew she would not be forgotten by our generation of children.'

Joe attempted to cheer her up. 'Did I ever tell you that your eyes are the colour of yellow-hammers' eggs? I was joking, of course.'

'No, Joe,' said Val wide-eyed. 'You never told me that, not even in fun.'

'Come on, I'll take you to see them.' He led her along a narrow path and paused just within sight of a gorse bush.

'I never knew yellow-hammers were so pretty,' breathed the girl staring. 'And what a lovely home they have, here in The Secret Wood.'

Their reverie was broken by Angela and Cyril

who came skidding up on their bikes. 'Billy is going to be enormously rich,' they gasped. 'Our dad has examined his ancient sovereigns and reckons they're worth a fortune!' then they rode off again.

'Well, fancy that,' smiled Joe as they strolled to the old stone bridge. 'Now Billy can take Mum on the world cruise Dad promised her.'

'Doesn't the stream look beautiful in the setting sun and the mist,' said the girl, leaning and gazing down. Joe joined her.

'We nearly lost all this,' he said. 'The bridge, the stream, The Secret Wood, perhaps even The Dingles itself. Thanks to us pulling together we've saved it all.'

'Not forgetting poor Gertie Crabtree and her father who died so many years ago,' added Val. 'Now she can rest in peace. Her sad ghost need never wander The Secret Wood again.'

'We mustn't forget Mr Hopkins,' grinned Joe. 'Fancy him helping us to keep our land, completely without charge. He's a good bloke really. You know, I'm getting this picture of an important solicitor and our Billy talking coins, swapping them, even. Though Mr Hopkins will need to be sharp to pull one over my brother, many have found that out.'

'I wouldn't be surprised if they aren't firm friends by now,' smiled Val. 'A shared passion for collecting can break down the highest barriers.'

'I can just imagine Mr Hopkins and Billy fighting over who gets the first go of the metal-detector,' Joe laughed.

'About the tigers in The Dingles, Joe,' said Val, changing the subject and looking at him carefully. 'Have you ever believed in them?'

'Well,' said Joe, slowly. 'It's probably a question of faith. My mum told me that generations of kids have swore to seeing tigers here. I'll admit I've never seen one myself.'

'I have,' said Val, suddenly. 'The day of the fight on the bridge, I saw one then. Its eyes were flashing and its claws were bared as it prepared to pounce in defence of its territory.'

'I didn't see that,' said Joe, astonished.

'How could you,' said Val, bursting into peels of laughter. 'For that tiger was you, Joe Crabtree – and now it's time to go home.'

They had one last good look at The Secret Wood as dusk descended. Joe's owl flew in to perch on a branch above the stream and bridge. It hooted softly, its saucer eyes intent on the pair. The boy and the girl hooted back. Satisfied, the bird flitted away into The Secret Wood, quickly swallowed by the dark trees. Turning, Joe walked Val back home along the narrow treacherous paths, through the spine-tingling tiger-grass and through the gap in the hawthorn hedge. The street-lamps and the damp pavements seemed so alien after the soft-treading, starry place they had just left. But The Dingles and The Secret Wood would always be there whenever they wished to return . . .

They said goodnight and parted. Both would sleep well till morning, their dreams a wonderful mix of the past, the present and the future . . .